THE

PRACTICE

OF

COURTS MARTIAL.

BY

ALEXANDER MACOMB,

MAJOR-GENERAL OF THE ARMY OF THE UNITED STATES.

THE LAWBOOK EXCHANGE, LTD.
Clark, New Jersey
2008

ISBN-13: 978-1-58477-887-5
ISBN-10: 1-58477-887-3

The quality of this reprint is equivalent to the quality of the original work.

THE LAWBOOK EXCHANGE, LTD.
33 Terminal Avenue
Clark, New Jersey 07066-1321

Please see our website for a selection of our other publications and fine facsimile reprints of classic works of legal history:
www.lawbookexchange.com

Library of Congress Cataloging-in-Publication Data

Macomb, Alexander, 1782-1841.
The practice of courts martial / by Alexander Macomb.
p. cm.
Previously published: New York : Printed by Harper & brothers, 1841.
Includes bibliographical references and index.
ISBN-13: 978-1-58477-887-5 (cloth : alk. paper)
ISBN-10: 1-58477-887-3 (cloth : alk. paper)
1. Courts-martial and courts of inquiry--United States. I. Title.
KF7625.M32 2008
343.73'0143--dc22

2008003777

Printed in the United States of America on acid-free paper

THE

PRACTICE

OF

COURTS MARTIAL.

BY

ALEXANDER MACOMB,

MAJOR-GENERAL OF THE ARMY OF THE UNITED STATES.

NEW-YORK:

PRINTED BY HARPER & BROTHERS.

1841.

RECOMMENDATION.

It being of the first importance in the administration of justice, that the Officers of the Army should be acquainted with the principles and rules governing Military Courts, and that they should also have a competent knowledge of the laws and usages of the service; the War Department, in order to promote so desirable an end, recommends to the Military Service, "The Practice of Courts Martial, by Alexander Macomb, Major-general of the Army of the United States."

War Department,
February 19th, 1841.

(Signed) J. R. POINSETT.

CONTENTS.

APPENDIX.

INTRODUCTION.

THE discipline and reputation of the Army are deeply involved in the manner in which Military Courts are conducted, and justice administered. The duties, therefore, that devolve on officers who may be appointed to sit as members of Courts Martial, are of the most grave and important character: that these duties may be discharged with justice and propriety, it is incumbent on all officers to apply themselves diligently to the acquirement of a competent knowledge of Military law; to make themselves perfectly acquainted with the Acts of Congress relating to the Army and Militia, with the regulations and General Orders, and with the practice of Military Courts.

Military jurisprudence has, of late years, undergone considerable changes, and been much improved; consequently the practice of Courts Martial has experienced modifications to correspond with such improvement. A book, embracing the improved mode of proceeding in Courts Martial, whether General, or Regimental, including Courts of Inquiry, has been much sought after, especially one that could be regarded as a manual adapted to the use of the Army and Militia of the United States. This work is intended to be such a manual. It is not offered as an original production in all its parts; it is necessarily made up of the established opinions and practices of Courts Martial, as confirmed by general orders, and by the books of acknowledged accuracy in such matters.

To assist the members of Courts Martial in regard to the evidence proper to be received, and in weighing it when brought to their consideration, a synopsis of the general rules on that subject is introduced into the body of the work, without which the work itself would be incomplete.

There are also appended, forms of orders for appointing the various descriptions of Military Courts, and of recording their proceedings.

The author acknowledges himself under great obligations to the honorable Benjamin Franklin Butler, late Attorney-General of the United States, to whose inspection this work, in its original form, was submitted. After carefully perusing every paragraph, the Attorney-General made such amendments and additions as appeared to him proper, all which have been adopted. It may, therefore, be said, that the work has received the general approbation of that high functionary.

It will be a source of real pleasure to the author, if this work should prove to be such as to answer all the purposes for which it was intended, viz.: the introduction of a regular system of procedure in Courts Martial, and the maintenance of order and discipline in the service. It is a well-established fact, that the infrequency of Courts Martial is in proportion to the intelligence and well-regulated zeal of the Officers of the Army. It is as much a duty to prevent, as to punish crime. An officer may do much to this effect, by timely interference. A judicious intercourse with his men, gives him that knowledge of their characters, which enables him to admonish with equal benefit to them and advantage to the service. They should feel an assurance, that, while their rights are guarded, their offences will not go unpunished.

AUTHORITY OF COURTS MARTIAL.

§ 1. Courts Martial, whether in the Regular Army or Militia, derive their Authority from express acts of legislation, by Congress, or by the States individually composing the Union. And the laws in reference to such Courts, have the same positive obligation on those whom they are intended to bind, as the Common, or Statute law has, in cases coming within either, on the Citizens of the United States. The Military code is contained in the Act of Congress of the 10th of April, 1806, commonly called the Rules and Articles of War, and in other Acts and parts of Acts, which are appended to this work; to which might be added the general regulations, issued from the War Department. Courts Martial are either *General*, for the trial of the greater military crimes, or *Regimental*, or *Garrison*, for the cognizance of smaller offences.

GENERAL COURTS MARTIAL.

§ 2. General Courts Martial are the highest Military tribunals. Their jurisdiction is general, and extends over all the military offences committed by officers, non-commissioned officers, soldiers, and other individuals belonging to the Army and subject to Military Law. General Courts Martial, in the regular Army, are appointed by the authority of the President of the United States; or that of any general Officer commanding an Army, or Colonel commanding a separate department. [See Art. of War, 65.] But, whenever a general officer commanding an Army, or Colonel commanding a separate department, shall be the accuser, or prosecutor of any officer in the Army of the United States, under his command; the General Court Martial for the trial of such officer shall be appointed by the President of the United States. [See Act of 29th of May, 1830.] General Courts Martial in the Militia, when not called into the service of the United States, are appointed according to the Laws of the several States to which the Militia may respectively belong.

§ 3. General Courts Martial may consist of any number of Commissioned Officers from five to thirteen inclusively; but they must not consist of less than thirteen, when that number can be convened without manifest injury to the service. [See Art. of War, 64.]

§ 4. Commissioned officers here alluded to, are all officers holding commissions, from the rank of General to that of Ensign and Cornet, whether in the regular Army, Marine Corps, Militia, or Volunteers; but, the Militia are liable to be tried only by Courts Martial composed entirely of Militia officers. [See Art. of War, 97.]

§ 5. It is not customary, nor is it considered as coming within the rule, to place any officer on a Court Martial, as a member, who has no military rank, as Surgeons, Assistant-surgeons, Paymasters and the like, who, although Commissioned officers, are not subject to be detailed for such duty; they may, however, when the state of the service will admit of it, be appointed to do the duty of Judge Advocate.

§ 6. In ordering a Court Martial, it is not necessary, (though it may be done) to designate the President by name, as the officer highest in rank has the right to preside—that rank being determined by the Articles of War, applicable to that subject. [See Art. War, 61, 68, and 98.]

§ 7. In detailing officers to form a General Court Martial, it will be sufficient to order as many members as can be convened "*without manifest injury to the service*," within the limits mentioned in the 64th Article of War, of which the ordering officer must be the judge.

§ 8. The greatest number of officers that can be

convened, "*without manifest injury to the service*," will, in all cases, be ordered; but, on the appointed day of meeting, the Court may consider itself authorized to organize and act, when the number is not fixed, provided the number present does not fall short of five, unless otherwise ordered; as for instance, the Court may be ordered to consist of seven, nine, or some other number of members; in which case, the number of members fixed in the order, must be present, before the Court can be legally organized.

§ 9. When the Court is ordered to consist of thirteen members, it is proper, if it can be conveniently done, to order supernumerary officers to be detailed, to supply any vacancies that may occur, at the day of meeting, or at any subsequent day.

§ 10. But, when the number of officers detailed to form the Court, falls short of thirteen, there can be no *supernumeraries*—it is only when the maximum is exceeded, that the *term* properly applies. In case a vacancy should occur under such circumstances, the Commander of a contiguous post should be directed to supply an officer to sit as a member; for when the number is specified in the order, that number must be made good, or the Court cannot proceed.

§ 11. It is very proper to designate the rank of the officers who are to compose the Court, and the Regiments that are to furnish the members, according to the roster.

§ 12. When the officers are all present in camp, it is customary to name the President and members; but, when the Court is to assemble at a distant post, it is better to omit naming the President, leaving it to be determined by the rank of the officers present at the meeting of the Court; for, if the President be named in the order, and any accident prevent his attendance, the Court could not proceed until a communication to the officer who ordered the Court should be made, in order that another officer might be designated to supply the vacancy. Such delay might prove injurious to the service, and very painful and unjust to the prisoner to be tried.

§ 13. The seat of a member of a Court Martial, who is absent from a sufficient cause, is to be considered as permanently vacated, and is to be filled accordingly, either by a supernumerary or by an officer from a contiguous post.

§ 14. Officers assembled to constitute a Court Martial, may meet and adjourn, notwithstanding all the members may not be present, but no other act of theirs can be legal, without the presence of the whole Court, except in deciding on the validity of a challenge against a member; the member challenged usually withdrawing during the consideration of the challenge by the other members.

§ 15. The day and place of meeting of a Court Martial having been published in Orders, they are not to be changed, but by the authority which ordered the Court; and the officers appointed as members, the parties and witnesses, must attend accordingly.

§ 16. With the appointment or constitution of the Court, the authority of the officer who ordered the Court ceases, until that Court shall have pronounced judgment. He cannot interfere with its procedure, in the execution of its duty. The Court exists until it be dissolved by the authority which appointed it, or a higher authority.

THE ARREST IN ORDER TO TRIAL.

---

§ 17. Before an officer or soldier, or other person subject to Military law, can be brought to trial, he must be charged with some crime or offence, against the Rules and Articles of War, or good order and military discipline, and placed in arrest.

§ 18. The Articles of War direct that whenever any officer shall be charged with a crime, he shall be arrested and confined in his barracks, quarters, or tent, and deprived of his sword by the Commanding Officer. And that "non-commissioned officers and soldiers, charged with crimes, shall be confined until tried by a Court Martial, or released by proper authority." [See Art. War, 77 and 78.]

§ 19. The arrest of an officer is generally executed by the ministration of a Staff-Officer; as by an Adjutant, if ordered by the Commanding Officer of his Regiment; or by an officer of the General Staff, if ordered by his superior officer; and sometimes by the officer himself, with whom the arrest originates. On being placed in arrest, an officer resigns his sword to the person executing it. If this form be sometimes omitted, it is nevertheless considered to have taken place, and hence originates the custom, which is invariably observed, that an officer in arrest appears without a sword.

§ 20. Although the Articles of War make no mention of any difference in the nature of the arrest in order to trial, still, a difference is established by the custom of the Army, according to the degree or measure of the crime. An officer accused of a Capital crime, or any offence of which the penalty is so severe as to excite a natural temptation to escape from justice, ought to be detained in a state of confinement, as secure as the closest civil imprisonment. If the offence be of a lighter nature, the presumption is, that the officer whose character is thus impeached, must be solicitous to obtain a judicial investigation of his conduct, and he is, therefore, generally allowed to be in arrest at large; that is, without his sword, on his word of honor, to await the issue of a trial, or his enlargement by proper authority. The degree and measure of the arrest must, however, be entirely at the discretion of the Commanding Officer, who will, in all cases, regulate his conduct by the particular circumstances, and by the dictates of propriety and humanity.

§ 21. A non-commissioned officer or soldier is confined in charge of a guard; but, by the custom of the service, the non-commissioned staff and sergeants, are frequently only placed in close arrest.

§ 22. The Articles of War declare, "that no officer or soldier, who shall be put in arrest or imprisonment, shall continue in his confinement more than eight days, or until such time as a Court Martial can be conveniently assembled." [See Art. of War, 79.] The latter part of this clause evidently allows a latitude, which is capable of being abused; but, as in a free country there is no wrong without a remedy, the military law points out a mode of redress for all officers or soldiers, who conceive themselves injured by their Commanding Officer, which must always be sufficient for restraining every act of injustice or oppression. [See Art. of War, 34 and 35.]

§ 23. It is declared, by the Articles of War, that "no officer commanding a guard or provost-marshall, shall refuse to receive or keep any prisoner committed to his charge, by any officer belonging to the forces of the United States; provided, the officer committing shall, at the same time, deliver an account in writing, signed by himself, of the crime with which the said prisoner is charged;" and it is also declared, that "no officer commanding a guard, or provost-marshall, shall presume to release any prisoner committed to his charge, without proper authority for so doing, nor shall he suffer any person to escape, on the penalty of being punished for it by the sentence of a Court Martial. Every officer or provost-marshall, to whose charge prisoners shall be committed, shall, within twenty-four hours after such commitment, or as soon as he shall be relieved from his guard, make report in writing, to the Commanding Officer, of their names, their crimes, and the names of the officers who committed them, on the penalty of being punished for disobedience or neglect, at the discretion of a Court Martial." [Art. of War, 80, 81, and 82.]

§ 24. Thus the liberty of the citizen, under military law, so far as is consistent with the ends of justice, seems to be guarded with precautions little inferior in their power and efficacy, to those which secure personal liberty under the civil laws of the state. The penalty of an officer's breaking his arrest, or leaving his confinement before he is set at liberty by his Commanding Officer, or by a superior officer, is declared to be cashiering by sentence of a General Court Martial. [Art. of War, 77.]

§ 25. A Court Martial has no control over the nature of the arrest of a prisoner, except as regards his personal freedom in Court; the Court cannot, even with a view to facilitate his defence, interfere to cause a close arrest to be enlarged. The officer in command is alone responsible for the prisoners under his charge.

§ 26. Individuals placed in arrest, may be released, without being brought before a Court martial; by the authority ordering the arrest, or by superior authority.

§ 27. It is not obligatory on the Commander to place an officer in arrest, on application to that effect from an officer under his command. He will exercise a sound discretion on the subject. But in all applications for redress of supposed grievances inflicted by a superior, it will be his duty, in case he shall not deem it proper to order an investigation, to give his reasons in writing, for declining to act; these reasons, if not satisfactory, the complaining party may, should he think fit so to do, forward to the next common superior, together with a copy of his application for redress.

§ 28. An officer has no right to demand a Court Martial, either on himself, or on others; the General-in-chief, or officer competent to order a Court, being the judge of its necessity or propriety.

§ 29. Nor has an officer, who may have been placed in arrest, any right to demand a trial, or to persist in considering himself under arrest, after he shall have been released by proper authority.

§ 30. An officer under arrest will not make a visit of etiquette to the Commanding Officer, or other superior officer, or call on him, unless sent for; and in case of business, he will make known his object in writing. It is considered indecorous in an officer in arrest, to appear at public places.

CHARGES OR ACCUSATION.

§ 31. A charge against an officer, or soldier, or other person, need not be framed with the technical formalities, which prevail in other Courts of Law; but, in whatever terms a charge may be expressed, it must set forth the crime or offence in a manner sufficiently specific, to enable the person accused to know to what he is to answer, and the Court, into what it is called to inquire. Charges, therefore, must designate the prisoner by his name, surname, rank, and the Regiment or department of the Army, to which he belongs. The fact or facts ought also to be distinctly specified or alleged, in such a manner, that neither the prisoner nor the Court can have any difficulty in knowing what is the precise object of the trial. The same minuteness and precision ought to be observed in specifying the time and place, when and where, the facts charged were committed, for such specification may be essentially necessary to the prisoner's defence. But, if a doubt be entertained, as to the precise time and place, it may be set forth in a charge, that the fact was committed at or near such a place, and on or about such a date. This, however, ought never to be permitted, if it can possibly be avoided without a sacrifice of justice, as it may deprive the prisoner of many advantages on his defence.

§ 32. Facts distinct in their nature, are not to be included in one and the same charge, or specification of a charge, but must be the subject of a distinct charge or specification.

§ 33. All extraneous matter is to be carefully avoided, and nothing is to be alleged but that which is culpable, and which the complainant is prepared to substantiate, before a Court Martial.

§ 34. It is not necessary to specify in a charge, that the offence alleged was committed in breach of any particular Article of War.

§ 35. A charge is not necessarily to be laid before a Court Martial in the form in which it has been drawn up by the complainant; the officer who may order the Court to assemble, being competent to make such alterations in it as he may deem requisite.

§ 36. But, after a charge has been approved by the proper authority and ordered to be investigated, neither the Judge Advocate, nor any other person is competent to change it, without the consent of such authority.

§ 37. It is highly improper to hold charges in reserve against an officer or soldier, in order that they may accumulate, so as to form collectively a crime of sufficient magnitude to justify a prosecution. If the facts as they arise, are not fit to be made matters of charge at the time they become known, they should never, but in extraordinary cases, be subsequently revived.

§ 38. It is customary to furnish the accused with a copy of the charge or charges to be preferred against him, some time before the trial, and though the prisoner cannot plead the deviation from this custom, or any discordance between the copy given him and that exhibited before the Court as a bar to trial; yet, the Court, under such circumstances and particularly where the deviation may be material, would probably deem it a sufficient cause for delaying proceedings; as common sense and justice would dictate, that the accused should have a knowledge of the accusations brought against him, previous to trial, and that adequate time be afforded him to meet the charges, by such evidence and reasoning as the case may require, and as he may deem expedient.

§ 39. No person shall be liable to be tried and punished, by a General Court Martial, for any offence which shall appear to have been committed more than two years before the issuing of the order for such trial, unless the person by reason of having absented himself, or some other manifest impediment, shall not have been amenable to justice within that period. [See Art. of War, 88.]

THE TRIAL.

---

§ 40. All trials before Courts Martial, like those in the civil courts of judicature, are conducted publicly and with open doors; and in order that this publicity of trial may in no case be attended with tumult or indecorum of any kind, the Court is authorized, by the Rules and Articles of War, to punish at its discretion, all riotous and disorderly proceedings, or menacing words, signs or gestures, used in its presence. [See Art. of War, 76.]

§ 41. The day and place of meeting of a General Court Martial having been published in orders, they shall not be changed, but by the authority ordering the same; and the officers appointed as members, the parties and witnesses, must attend accordingly. The Judge Advocate, at the opening, calls over the names of the members, who arrange themselves on the right or left of the President, according to their rank as settled by the Articles of War. [See Art. of War, 61.]

§ 42. The members of the Court having taken their seats and disposed of any preliminary matter, the prisoner, prosecutor and witnesses, are called into Court. The prisoner is attended by a guard, or by an officer, as his rank or the nature of the charge may dictate. The prisoner, during the trial, should be without irons, unfettered and free from any bonds or shackles, unless there be danger of escape or rescue.

§ 43. Accommodation is usually afforded, at detached tables, for the prosecutor and prisoner; also for any friend or legal adviser of the prisoner or prosecutor, the benefit of whose assistance they may, respectively, desire during the trial. Though the parties only are permitted to address the Court, it being an admitted maxim, in military Courts, that counsel are not to interfere in the proceedings or to offer the slightest remark, much less to plead or argue, yet a prisoner or prosecutor is not precluded the advantage of their presence and advice.

§ 44. The Judge Advocate, by direction of the President, first reads, in an audible voice, the warrant order for holding the Court. He then calls over the names of the members, commencing with the President, who is always the highest in rank, and so descending to the youngest member.

§ 45. The Judge Advocate then demands of the prisoner, whether he has any exception or cause of challenge against any of the members present, and if he have, he is required to state his cause of challenge, confining his challenge to one member at a time. [See Art. of War, 71.] After hearing the prisoner's objections, the President must order the Court to be cleared, when the members will deliberate on and determine the relevancy or validity of the same; the member challenged usually retiring during the discussion.

§ 46. It may be proper here to state, that all deliberations by a Court Martial, are held with closed doors. The President orders the Court to be cleared for deliberation, when he may deem it necessary, or for any incidental discussion, at the instance of a member, or the Judge Advocate.

§ 47. Sufficient causes for challenge are:—the expression of an opinion relative to the subject to be investigated; having been a member of a Court of Inquiry which gave an opinion; or of another General Court Martial, in which the circumstances were directly investigated; or of another General Court Martial in which the circumstances were investigated incidentally and an opinion formed thereon; prejudice, malice or the like.

§ 48. The privilege of challenge is mutual to the prisoner and to the prosecutor; for there may be sources of prejudice in favor of the prisoner as well as against him, and urgent motives that may sway to acquit, as well as condemn.

§ 49. When the prisoner and prosecutor decline to challenge any of the members, or where the causes of challenge have been disallowed, the Judge Advocate proceeds to administer to the members of the Court, the oath prescribed by the 69th Article of War, which is in the following words: "You, A. B. do swear, that you will well and truly try and determine, according to evidence, the matter now before you, between the United States of America and the prisoner to be tried; and that you will duly administer justice according to the provisions of 'an act establishing rules and articles for the government of the Armies of the United States,' without partiality, favor or affection: and if any doubt shall arise, not explained by said articles, according to your understanding and the custom of War in like cases: and you do further swear, that you will not divulge the sentence of the Court, until it shall be published by the proper authority: neither will you disclose or discover the vote or opinion of any particular member of the Court Martial, unless required to give evidence thereof, as a witness, by a Court of Justice in a due course of law. So help you God." The oath is taken by each member holding up his right hand and repeating the words after the Judge Advocate. After the oath has been administered to all the members, the President administers to the Judge Advocate, the particular oath of secrecy to be observed by him, and which, as prescribed by Article 69, is as follows: "You, A. B. do swear that you will not disclose or discover the vote or opinion of any particular member of the Court Martial, unless required to give evidence thereof as a witness, by a Court of Justice in due course of law, nor divulge the sentence of the Court to any but the proper authority, until it shall be duly disclosed by the same. So help you God."

§ 50. The oath taken by the President and members contains a twofold obligation to secrecy: 1st, That they will not divulge the sentence of the Court, until it shall be published by proper authority; and,

2d, That they shall not disclose or discover the vote or opinion of any particular member of the Court Martial, unless required to give evidence thereof by a Court of Justice, in a due course of law. Both these obligations have their foundation in reason and good policy.

§ 51. No sentence of a General Court Martial is complete or final, until it has been duly approved. Until that period it is, strictly speaking, no more than an opinion, which is subject to alteration or revisal. In this interval, the communication of that opinion could answer no ends of justice, but might, in many cases, tend to frustrate them. The obligation to perpetual secrecy, with regard to the votes or opinions of the particular members of the Court, is likewise founded on the wisest policy. The members of a Court Martial cannot boast of the same independence of the Executive, and consequent immunity from influence, as the Judges in the ordinary Courts of Law. The officers who compose a Military tribunal are, in a great degree, dependent for their preferment on the President and the Secretary of War. They are even in some measure under the influence of their Commander-in-Chief; powerful considerations which might sometimes lead a weaker mind astray from the direct paths of justice. This danger is therefore best obviated, by the confidence and security which every member possesses, that his particular opinion is never to be divulged. Another reason of yet stronger nature, is, that the individual members of the Court may not be exposed to the resentment of parties and their connections, which can hardly fail to be excited by those sentences, which it is often obligatory on Courts Martial to award. It may be necessary for officers, in the course of their duty, daily, to associate and frequently to be sent on the same command or service, with a person against whom they have given an unfavorable vote or opinion on a Court Martial. The publicity of these votes or opinions would create the most dangerous animosities, equally fatal to the peace and security of individuals, and prejudicial to the public service.

§ 52. The oath which is taken by the Judge Advocate, contains the same obligation to secrecy, except so far as it relates to the person who has the approving or disapproving of the sentence of the Court. It is not inconsistent with his oath or duty, for the Judge Advocate to communicate to the proper authority, his views of the proceedings of the Court.

§ 53. The Judge Advocate is, however, bound by oath, as well as the members of the Court, to maintain the strictest secrecy with regard to the votes or opinions of individuals, for the same reasons of expediency and sound policy as above stated.

§ 54. When more prisoners than one are to be arraigned before the same Court Martial, for distinct offences, the members are liable to be challenged and the Court is to be sworn, *de novo*, at the commencement of each case; and the proceedings are to be made up separately and signed, as if each prisoner had been tried by a distinct Court Martial.

§ 55. The oath taken by the members of the Court

commences with these words: "You, A. B. do swear that you will well and truly try and determine, according to evidence, the matter now before you, between the United States of America and the prisoner to be tried." [See Art. of War, 69.] The expression, "prisoner," in the singular number, seems rather to imply that the swearing, and consequently the trial, should in each case be separate. That course should be pursued in all cases, even where a joint offence is charged; except that persons charged with joint offences of a venial nature, and when the punishment is *slight*, may be tried together or separately at the discretion of the Court.

§ 56. Application to delay the assembling of the Court, from the absence or indisposition of the witnesses, the illness of the parties, or other cause, should be made, when practicable, to the authority convening the Court; but application to put off or suspend the trial, may be urged with a Court Martial, subsequent to the swearing of the members. It may be supported by affidavit, and the Court, in allowing it to prevail, must be satisfied, if the cause be absence of a witness, that the testimony proposed to be offered is material, and that the applicant cannot have substantial justice without it. The points, therefore, which each witness is intended to prove, must be set forth in the application, and it must also be shown that the absence of the witness is not attributable to any neglect of the applicant.

§ 57. A precise period of delay must be applied for, and it must be made to appear that there is reasonable expectation of procuring the attendance of the witness by the stated time; or, if the absence of a witness be attributed to his illness, a Surgeon, by *viva voce* testimony, or by affidavit, must state the inability of the witness to the Court, the nature of his disease, and the time which will probably elapse before the witness may be able to give his testimony.

§ 58. The Court must obviously be adjourned at any period of its proceedings, prior to the final close of the prosecution and defence, on satisfactory proof, by a medical officer, that the prisoner is in such a state, that actual danger to his health would arise from his attendance in Court; and where the prisoner is so ill as to render it probable that his inability to attend the Court will be of such continuance as to operate to the inconvenience of the service, either by the detention of the members of the Court from their regiments, or from other cause, the Court may be dissolved by the authority which convened it. Though the prisoner may have been arraigned, and the trial proceeded with, the prisoner, on recovery, would be amenable to trial by another Court.

§ 59. The illness of the prosecutor would, in few cases, justify the suspension of the trial, excepting, perhaps, for a very limited period; all prosecutions before Courts Martial being considered at the suit of the United States, or an individual State, as the case may be.

§ 60. The Court being regularly constituted, and every preliminary form gone through, the Judge Advocate, as prosecutor for the United States, desires the prisoner to listen to the charge or charges brought against him, which he reads with an audible voice, and then the prisoner is asked, whether he is guilty or not guilty of the matter of accusation.

§ 61. A prisoner before a Court Martial may object to the total want of specification in the charge, as to matter or time, where time is essential to fix the identity: thus, an officer being charged with conduct unbecoming an officer and a gentleman, or a soldier, with unsoldier-like conduct, without any mention of facts to which the allegation is meant to refer, may object to the same as a reason for not answering. But, though it be admitted to have full effect in preventing the trial of the prisoner, upon the charge objected to, it cannot have the effect of barring trial upon any valid charge, wherein facts may be set forth. The prisoner's objection to the charge, if admitted, would be so upon the ground that the charge was couched in terms so vague, as not to point to any specific crime, to meet which, he might direct his attention. If, then, he were arraigned upon another charge, and by virtue of a different order, he could not, consistently, plead that he had been previously arraigned for the same offence, nor, if he did, could he hope to establish the plea.

§ 62. Where the essential requisites of the offence are distinctly specified, though in general terms, objections to the charge for want of sufficient minuteness, should be made before pleading; since the course of the prosecution will identify the facts to which the charge was meant to apply, and, therefore, exempt the prisoner from subsequent trial on charges built on these facts, as none can be tried twice for the same offence. [See 87, Art. of War.] There can be no doubt, that the total want of specification in the charge, may be urged not only as a legitimate reason for declining all defence, but also after a defence be made, as a ground for acquitting the prisoner, and that such a defect would render the proceedings nugatory, or rather innoxious to the prisoner, since no sentence of the Court under such circumstances could be maintained. But minor objections of this nature, which would be sufficient to excuse the prisoner from answering the charge, will be cured by his entering on his defence without making the objection *in limine.*

§ 63. The charge being sufficient, or not objected to, the prisoner must plead either:

1st. Guilty, or

2d. Specially to the jurisdiction, or in bar, or

3d. The general plea of *not guilty*, which is the usual course where the prisoner makes a defence.

§ 64. If from obstinacy and design the prisoner stand mute, or answer foreign to the purpose, the Court may proceed to trial and judgment, as if the prisoner had regularly pleaded *not guilty;* [See Art. of War, 70.] but if the prisoner plead *guilty*, the Court will proceed to determine what punishment shall be awarded, and to pronounce sentence thereon. Preparatory to this, in all cases where the punishment of the offence charged is discretionary, and especially where the discretion includes a wide range and great variety of punishment, and the specifications do not show all the circumstances attending the offence, the Court should receive and report, in its proceedings, any evidence the Judge Advocate may offer, for the purpose of illustrating the actual character of the offence, notwithstanding the party accused may have pleaded guilty; such evidence being necessary to an enlightened exercise of the discretion of the Court, in measuring the punishment, and also to those whose duty it may be to report on the case, or to carry the sentence into effect. If there be any exception to this rule, it is where the specification is so full and precise, as to disclose all the circumstances of mitigation or aggravation which accompany the offence. When that is the case, or when the punishment is fixed, and no discretion is allowed, explanatory testimony cannot be needed.

§ 65. Special pleas are either to the jurisdiction of the Court, or in bar of the charge. If a soldier be arraigned before an inferior Court Martial for a crime declared by the Articles of War to be cognizable by a Court Martial of superior jurisdiction, such authority not having been extended to the inferior Court; or if an officer or soldier be arraigned by a Court not legally constituted, either as to the authority by which it is assembled, or as to the number and rank of its members, for these and similar causes, a prisoner may except to the jurisdiction of the Court Martial.

§ 66. Special pleas in bar go to the merits of the case, and set forth a reason why, even admitting the charge to be true, it should be dismissed, and the prisoner discharged.

§ 67. A former acquittal or conviction of the same offence would obviously be a valid bar, except in case of appeal from a Regimental to a General Court Martial.

§ 68. It may be pleaded in bar that the offence charged had taken place more than two years before the issuing of the order for trial, unless the person accused by reason of having absented himself, or of some other manifest impediment, may not have been amenable to justice within that period; in which case, the plea would be valid only, if time, exceeding two years, had elapsed from the period when the impediment may have ceased. [Art. of War, 88.]

§ 69. Though the facts in issue should be charged to have happened more than two years prior to the date of the order for the assembling of the Court Martial, yet it is not the province of the Court, no objection being taken to the order for assembling the Court, to inquire into the cause of the impediment in the outset. It would be to presume the illegality of the Court, whereas, the Court should assume that manifest impediment to earlier trial did exist, and leave the facts to be developed by witnesses in the ordinary course.

§ 70. A pardon may be pleaded in bar. If full, it at once destroys the end and purpose of charge, by remitting that punishment which the prosecution is calculated to inflict; if conditional, the performance of the condition must be known; thus, a soldier arraigned for desertion, must plead a general pardon, and prove that he surrendered himself within the stipulated period.

§ 71. No officer or soldier, being acquitted or convicted of an offence, is liable to be tried a second time for the same. But this provision applies solely to trials for the same incidental act and crime, and to such persons as have, in the first instance, been legally tried. If any irregularity take place on the trial rendering it illegal and void, the prisoner must be discharged, and be regarded as standing in the same situation as before the commencement of these illegal proceedings. The same charge may, therefore, be again preferred against the prisoner, who cannot plead the previous illegal trial in bar.

§ 72. A prisoner cannot plead in bar that he has not been furnished with a copy of the charges, or that the copy furnished him differed from that on which he has been arraigned. It is customary and proper to furnish him with a correct copy; but, the omission shall not make void, though it may postpone the trial.

§ 73. If the special plea in bar, be such that, if true, the charge should be dismissed and the prisoner discharged, the Judge Advocate should be called on to answer it. If he does not admit it to be true, the prisoner must produce evidence to the points alleged therein; and if, on deliberation, the plea be found true, the facts being recorded, the Court will adjourn and the President submit the proceedings to the officer by whose order the Court was convened, with a view to the immediate discharge of the prisoner.

§ 74. The ordinary plea is *not guilty*, in which case the trial proceeds. The Judge Advocate cautions all witnesses on the trial to withdraw, and to return to Court, only on being called. He then proceeds to the examination of witnesses, and to the reading and proof of any written evidence he may have to bring forward.

§ 75. After a prisoner has been arraigned on specific charges, it is irregular for a Court Martial to admit any additional charge against him, even though he may not have entered on his defence. The trial on the charges first preferred, must be regularly concluded, when, if necessary, the prisoner may be tried on any further accusation brought against him.

§ 76. On the trial of cases not capital, before Courts Martial, the deposition of witnesses not in the Line or Staff of the Army, may be taken before some justice of the peace, and read in evidence, provided, the prosecutor and person accused are present at the same, or are duly notified thereof.

§ 77. The examination of witnesses is invariably in the presence of each member of the Court; because, the countenance, looks, and gestures of a witness, add to, or take away from, the weight of his testimony. It is usually by interrogation, sometimes by narration; in either case, the Judge Advocate records the evidence, as nearly as possible, in the express words of the witness. All evidence, whatever, should be recorded on the proceedings, in the order in which it is received by the Court.

§ 78. A question, being reduced to writing by the

individual originating it, whether it be by the Judge Advocate, prosecutor, prisoner, or by a member of the Court, is passed to the President; if approved by him, it is read aloud, entered by the Judge Advocate on the proceedings, and, no objection being made to it by the opposite party, or the Court, it is then addressed to the witness. Should the President object to the question, he returns it for consideration to the person proposing it; if persisted in by such person, or if, on enunciation, it be objected to by a party, before the Court, by a member, or by the witness under examination, the Court is cleared and proceeds to determine, by a majority of votes, whether it shall be put or rejected.

§ 79. A question to a witness is registered before enunciation; when once entered, it cannot be expunged, except by the consent of the parties before the Court; if not permitted to be put to the witness, it still appears on the proceedings accompanied by the decision of the Court.

§ 80. The examination in chief of each particular witness being ended, the cross-examination usually follows, though it is optional with the prisoner to defer it to the final close of the examination in chief. The re-examination by the prosecutor, on such new points as the prisoner may have touched on, succeeds the cross-examination, and finally, the Court puts such questions as in its judgment may tend to elicit the truth.

§ 81. It is customary, when deemed necessary by the Court, or desired by a witness, to read over to him, immediately before he leaves the Court, the record of his evidence, which he is desired to correct if erroneous, and, with this view, any remark or explanation is entered upon the proceedings. No erasure or obliteration is, however, admitted, as it is essentially necessary that the authority which has to review the sentence, should have the most ample means of judging, not only of any discrepancy in the statements of a witness, but of any incident which may be made the subject of remark, by either party in addressing the Court.

§ 82. Although a list of witnesses, summoned by the Judge Advocate, is furnished to the Court on assembling, it is not held imperative on the prosecutor to examine such witness; if he should not do so, however, the prisoner has a right to call any of them.

§ 83. Should the prisoner, having closed his cross-examination, think proper subsequently to recall a prosecutor's witness, in his defence, the examination is held to be in chief, and the witness is subject to cross-examination by the prosecutor.

§ 84. Although either party may have concluded his case, or the regular examination of a witness, yet should a material question have been omitted, it is usually submitted by the party to the President, for the consideration of the Court, which generally permits it to be put.

§ 85. The prisoner being placed on his defence, to arrange and prepare which, he is, should he desire it, usually allowed a certain time, (perhaps a day or two, or more,) subsequently to the closing of the prosecution, he may proceed at once to the examination of witnesses; firstly, to meet the charge, and secondly to speak as to character, reserving his address to the Court, until the conclusion of such examination.

§ 86. The prisoner, having finished the examination in chief of each witness, the prosecution cross-examines; the prisoner re-examines, to the extent allowed to the prosecutor, that is, on such new points as the cross-examination may have touched on, and the Court puts any questions deemed necessary.

§ 87. The prisoner, having finally closed his examination of witnesses, and selecting this period to address the Court, offers such statement or argument as he may deem conducive to weaken the force of the prosecution, by placing his conduct in the most favorable light, accounting for, or palliating facts, confuting or removing any imputation as to motives; answering the arguments of the prosecutor, contrasting, comparing and commenting on, any contradictory evidence; summing up the evidence on both sides, where the result promises to favor the defence, and, finally, presenting his deductions therefrom.

§ 88. The utmost liberty consistent with the interest of parties not before the Court and with the respect due to the Court itself, should, at all times, be allowed a prisoner. As he has an undoubted right to impeach, by evidence, the character of the witnesses brought against him, so he is justified in contrasting and remarking on their testimony, and on the motives by which they, or the prosecutor, may have been influenced. All coarse and insulting language is, however, to be avoided, nor ought invective to be indulged in, as the most pointed defence may be couched in the most decorous language.

§ 89. The Court will prevent the prisoner from adverting to parties not before the Court, or only alluded to in evidence, further than may be actually necessary to his own exculpation.

§ 90. It may sometimes happen, that the party accused may find it absolutely necessary, in defence of himself, to throw blame and even criminality on others, who are no parties to the trial; nor can a prisoner be refused that liberty, which is essential to his own justification. It is sufficient for the party aggrieved, that the law can furnish ample redress against all calumnious or unjust accusations. The Court is bound to hear whatever address, in his defence, the accused may think fit to offer, not being in itself contemptuous or disrespectful.

§ 91. It is competent to a Court, if it think proper, to caution the prisoner, as he proceeds, that, in its opinion, such a line of defence as he may be pursuing would probably not weigh with the Court, nor operate in his favor; but, to decide against hearing him state arguments, which, notwithstanding such caution, he might persist in putting forward, as grounds of justification, or extenuation, (such arguments not being illegal in themselves,) is going beyond what any Court would be warranted in doing.

§ 92. It occasionally happens, that on presenting to the Court a written address, the prisoner is unequal to the task of reading it, from indisposition or nervous excitement; on such occasions, the Judge Advocate is sometimes requested by the President to read it; but, as the impression which might be anticipated to be made by it, may, in the judgment of the prisoner, be affected more or less by the manner of its delivery, Courts Martial generally feel disposed to concede to the accused, the indulgence of permitting it to be read by any friend named by him, particularly, if that friend be a military man, or if the Judge Advocate be the actual prosecutor.

§ 93. Courts Martial are particularly guarded in adhering to the custom which obtains, of resisting every attempt on the part of counsel to address them. A lawyer is not recognised by a Court Martial, though his presence is tolerated, as a friend of the prisoner, to assist him by advice in preparing questions for witnesses, in taking notes, and shaping his defence.

§ 94. The prisoner having closed his defence, the prosecutor is entitled to reply, when witnesses have been examined on the defence, or where new facts are opened in the address. Thus, though no evidence may be brought forward by the prisoner, yet should he advert to any case, and, by drawing a parallel, attempt to draw his justification from it, the prosecutor will be permitted to observe on the case so cited. When the Court allows the prosecutor to reply, it generally grants him a reasonable time to prepare it; and upon his reading it, the trial ceases.

§ 95. Should the prisoner have examined witnesses to points not touched on in the prosecution, or should he have entered on an examination impeaching the credibility of the prosecutor's evidence, the prosecutor is allowed to examine witnesses to the new matter; the Court being careful to confine him within the limits of this rule, which extends to the re-establishing the character of his witnesses, to impeaching those of the defence, and to rebutting the new matter brought forward by the prisoner, supported by evidence. He cannot be allowed to examine on any points, which, in their nature, he might have foreseen previously to the defence of the prisoner.

§ 96. The prosecutor will not be permitted to bring forward evidence to rebut or counteract the effect of matter elicited by his own cross-examination; this privilege being strictly confined, as before observed, to new matter introduced by the prisoner, and supported by his examination in chief. A defence, resting on motives, or qualifying the imputation attaching to facts, generally lets in evidence in reply, as, in such cases, the prisoner usually adverts, by evidence, to matter which it would have been impossible for the prosecutor to anticipate. The admissibility of evidence, in reply, may generally be determined by the answer to the questions: Could the prosecutor have foreseen this? Is it evidently new matter? Is the object of the further inquiry to re-establish the character of the witnesses impeached by evidence (not by declamation) in the course of the defence, or is it to impeach the character of the prisoner's witnesses?

§ 97. Cross-examination of such new witnesses, to

an extent limited by the examination in chief, that is, confined to such points or matter as the prosecutor shall have examined on, is allowed on the part of the prisoner, to whom, where witnesses are introduced in the reply, a rejoinder is permitted; wherein, by argument and deduction, he may endeavor to invalidate their effect; to which object he is to be strictly confined; but, the prisoner is not permitted to call further evidence, except to re-establish the credit of such witnesses, as may, by the prosecutor's witnesses in his reply, have been impugned. To an extent, limited by the argument of the prisoner, the prosecutor is allowed a second reply, or sur-rejoinder, as it is sometimes called. It is a rule in Military Courts, as in most Civil Courts, that the party which begins to maintain the issue, should conclude.

GENERAL RULES OF EVIDENCE.

---

§ 98. Evidence ought to be confined to the point at issue. Every proof ought to bear directly or indirectly upon the facts in dispute.

§ 99. The substance only need be proved.

§ 100. The affirmative of the issue ought to be proved by the affirming party.

§ 101. The best evidence to be had should be produced, still the substance only need be proved by such best evidence.

§ 102. A Court Martial judges as to the legality of evidence, as well as to the credit due to it.

§ 103. Direct or positive evidence, is that given by witnesses who speak from actual and immediate knowledge.

Presumptive, or circumstantial evidence, is that which is not direct and positive. The fact in question is inferred, and is deemed to be proved, on proof of circumstances which, as reason and experience teach us, usually attend such fact.

Circumstantial evidence has, in some instances, been found to produce much stronger assurance of guilt, than the most direct and positive.

As a general rule, positive evidence, from a creditable eye-witness, is the most satisfactory that can be produced; and the feeling of mankind inclines to it, in preference to that which is merely circumstantial.

§ 104. Where the issue is upon the life or death of a person, the proof of the fact lies with the party who asserts the death; for the presumption is, that he continues alive till the contrary be proved. But, where no account can be given of the person, this presumption of being alive ceases at the expiration of seven years from the time he was last known to be living.

§ 105. Confirmatory evidence, where accomplices are admitted against or for the prisoner. It is not necessary to confirm every part of their evidence; but so much of it should be confirmed, by clear and unimpeachable evidence, from others, as to satisfy the Court of the fairness and integrity of the evidence.

§ 106. Hearsay. It is a general rule that all evidence produced against a person should be in his presence, to give the benefit of cross-examining the witness, and should be on oath. Hearsay evidence is therefore not admissible.

§ 107. Dying declarations, made under the apprehension of immediate death, are evidence in cases of homicide, for the purpose of proving how, and by whom it was committed.

§ 108. Handwriting may be proved by any person well acquainted with it, who has seen the party write, or corresponded with him. Comparison of handwriting, as a general rule, is inadmissible against a prisoner, but may sometimes be received in his defence.

§ 109. Public written evidence is received on proof of the handwriting of the officer signing the document, or on proof of a sworn copy.

§ 110. Private written evidence in the hands of defendant. Notice to produce it should be given to defendant; he may refuse it, whereupon the prosecutor may produce an examined copy, or give parole evidence of the contents.

§ 111. Affidavits, to be received as such, must be proved by parole evidence to have been duly sworn; but, they may be received as admissions of the deponents, upon proof of their handwriting.

§ 112. Letters are proved by calling the writer, or by proving the handwriting by another.

§ 113. Official Military papers, Reports, Returns, &c., are admitted without the same strict rules of proof required in Courts of Common Law. And so are copies attested by the Adjutant General, or by any other proper officer of the department.

§ 114. Initials. If a man write a letter, and his handwriting be proved, though he sign only his initials, it is sufficient; or, if he enclosed such a paper, and the envelope were signed with his name in full; or, if by any other evidence it be traced to him, it is evidence.

§ 115. Presence with other actors, during part of

their acts, a general concert between all being established, will make the parties so present, liable with the actual perpetrators.

§ 116. Evidence, implicating third persons, if necessary for the prosecution or defence, should be admitted; the Court is not answerable for the result. It is the Court's paramount duty to examine all necessary evidence.

§ 117. The prisoner's bad character ought not to be given in evidence against him, unless to rebut evidence of good character produced by him. Nor can it be shown that the prisoner has a general disposition to commit the same kind of offence as that charged against him. Nor can it be proved that he has committed such offences before, unless the *scienter* is in question, when such evidence is admissible to prove it, the fact charged being first proved.

§ 118. Examination of a witness should be in a courteous manner; neither tedious nor vexatious, nor should he be asked why he recollects so much for one side, and so little for the other. Cross-examination should not be carried too far.

§ 119. Irrelevant and extraneous matter should be thrown out.

§ 120. Who may be witnesses. All persons having the use of understanding, and believing in a Supreme Being who will punish false swearing, are admissible and competent witnesses, unless disqualified, by conviction and judgment, for an infamous crime, or by interest in the subject matter of inquiry.

§ 121. Idiots and, during the influence of their

frenzy, madmen and lunatics, are incompetent to give evidence; but, during lucid intervals, lunatics may be examined. Persons deaf and dumb, if they be capable of communicating their ideas by signs, and have a due sense of the obligation of an oath, may be admitted as witnesses and examined, through the intervention of an interpreter. The competency of children depends not upon their age, for there is no fixed and settled age at which an infant may be sworn; but, upon the degree of knowledge and understanding which, upon examination, they appear to possess. Children cannot testify except upon oath, and it is, therefore, not their general acquirements, but their knowledge of religion and accountableness to God, which will determine their competency. It is usual to examine children of tender age, before the oath is administered to them.

§ 122. The testimony of one who has been convicted of a felony or any other species of *crimen falsi*, is regarded by the law as of too doubtful a character to be admitted in a Court of Justice.

§ 123. Some of the crimes which render incompetent, are: treason, felony, perjury, subornation of perjury, piracy, swindling, cheating, barratry and bribing a witness to absent himself and not give evidence, &c. It is the conviction, which renders the witness incompetent, and that must be proved by the record of the judgment; for, an admission of the conviction will not render the witness incompetent. The disability may be removed by pardon, except in perjury, or by reversal of judgment.

§ 124. Relationship, &c. No tie of relationship disqualifies, except that of husband and wife. It is an admitted rule that neither is competent for or against the other, in civil or criminal cases; even though divorced by law, if the subject of inquiry occurred during their connection. But, where neither is a party, nor directly interested in the inquiry, either is competent to prove any fact not tending directly to criminate the other. But the wife may, *ex-necessitate*, be a witness against the husband on a charge of violence committed on her person; and her dying declarations are, for the like reason, admissible against the husband in the case of murder.

§ 125. Exception to competency. It is now agreed, that if the ground of objection appear at any time during the trial, the witness shall be considered incompetent, and his evidence rejected.

§ 126. A list of witnesses for the prosecution should, in all practicable cases, be given to the prisoner; but, a prisoner cannot demand it as a right. Witnesses not in the list may be called.

§ 127. Prisoners may be brought from prison to give their evidence.

§ 128. Should the witness be sick, the whole Court may adjourn to his room.

§ 129. Members of the Court may be witnesses, and after testifying resume their seats.

FINDING AND SENTENCE.

§ 130. The last stage of a trial before a Court Martial, is the exercise by the Court of its judicial functions, in the return of a solemn verdict on the guilt or innocence of the prisoner, and pronouncing sentence; this is to be done with closed doors, after the parties and all indifferent persons have been ordered to withdraw.

§ 131. As the Court is now in possession of the whole evidence, which has been carefully reduced to writing by the Judge Advocate, as recorder of the Court, together with all arguments upon the evidence, both on the part of the prosecutor and the prisoner; it is customary, before proceeding to deliberate upon the judgment, that the Court should have the proceedings read over by the Judge Advocate, which answers the double purpose of bringing the whole body of the evidence, in one connected view, to the recollection of the members, and of ascertaining the accuracy and fidelity of the record, by comparing it with the notes taken by individual members, in the course of the trial.

§ 132. The duty of the Judge Advocate, at this stage of the proceedings, being simply to act as recorder of the Court, and to advise on legal points, when his opinion may be demanded, he will necessarily abstain from making any remarks, by which his judgment as to the guilt or innocence of the prisoner may be ascertained, or the opinions of the others affected.

§ 133. When there are distinct and separate charges, or articles of accusation, the members of the Court reason and deliberate separately on each charge; candidly discussing, in free and open conversation, the import of the evidence, and allowing its full weight to every argument or presumption in favor of the prisoner; and being thus ripe for the decision, the Judge Advocate, by direction of the President, puts the question of "guilty or not guilty" of each specification of the charge, and of the charge itself, to each of the members, beginning with the youngest, [See Art. of War, 72,] and so ascending to the President, and writing down from each member, his vote and opinion, for acquittal or conviction. The votes are then counted, and if the majority declare the prisoner not guilty, he is accordingly acquitted of such charge. It is humanely provided, in the 87th Art. of War, that no sentence of death shall be pronounced against any offender, unless two-thirds of the members shall concur in the sentence. In other cases, the Court passes judgment by the majority of voices; and should the Court consist of an even number and be equally divided, the prisoner is of course acquitted.

§ 134. If, on the other hand, the majority declare the prisoner guilty, the Court proceeds next to determine what punishment shall be awarded, and to pronounce sentence for its infliction. The opinions or votes of the members are taken, in this last question, in the same manner as on the former; nor are those members who have in the previous question voted for acquittal, to be debarred from voting on the second, which is to decide the nature or degree of the punishment; for it would be most unjust, that those who thought so favorably of the prisoner's case as to vote for absolute acquittal, should be prevented from voting for as mild a punishment as possible consistent with the nature of the crime of which he is found guilty. The members of a Court Martial are in the double capacity of jurors and judges; as jurors they find the facts, and as judges they award the punishment.

§ 135. The punishments which it is in the power of a Court Martial to inflict, are various in their nature and degree, from the highest, which is death, down to those of the lightest nature, as a short confinement for a private soldier, or reprimand for a Commissioned officer.

§ 136. In some particular cases, the Articles of War point out the express punishment to be awarded, as thus: "Every officer who shall be convicted before a General Court Martial, of having signed a false certificate, relating to the absence of either officer or private soldier, or relative to his or their pay, shall be cashiered." [See Art. of War, 14.] So likewise in case of an officer knowingly receiving a deserter from any other Corps, without confining him and giving notice to the regiment to which he formerly belonged. [See Art. of War, 22.] In such cases, the Court has no discretionary powers, but must pronounce the sentence which the law requires, wherever the fact is proved.

§ 137. There are but two instances in which capital sentences are decreed by the Articles of War, without a discretionary power of the Court of commuting the punishment. The one is contained in the 55th Article of War: "Whosoever belonging to the Armies of the United States, employed in foreign parts, shall force a safeguard, shall suffer death." The other is the 2d section, concerning spies, where it is enacted: "That in time of War, all persons not citizens of, or owing allegiance to the United States of America, who shall be found lurking as spies, in or about the fortifications or encampments of the Armies of the United States, or of any of them, shall suffer death, according to law and the usage of nations, by sentence of a General Court Martial."

§ 138. There are other crimes for the commission of which the Articles of War authorize the punishment of death; but, as these crimes may be of different degrees of atrocity, the Court, at its discretion, may award "*such other punishment*," as, by its sentence, it may think proper to inflict, according to the nature of the crime: but when the word *death* is omitted, it evidently implies, that the power of punishing capitally is excluded—indeed, it is positively so declared by the 87th Article of War.

It is to be observed, however, that this expression, "*such other punishment*," is to be limited by the custom of the service.

§ 139. The inferior punishments are various, according to the degree of the crimes and rank of the persons who committed them. Of those peculiar to the rank of Commissioned officers, the most severe of the inferior punishments is *cashiering;* that is, depriving an officer of his commission, breaking him, and taking from him his military character. This is sometimes done simply, that is, without carrying in the sentence and judgment against the offender, an incapacity to be restored afterwards to his military character; or with the addition of a judgment of Court, declaring the offender utterly unfit or disabled to have or to hold any office or employment in the service of the United States; [See Art. of War, 15 and 16,] which is the highest of the subordinate punishments that can be inflicted on a Commissioned officer.

§ 140. *Suspension from rank and pay*, deprives an officer of his military character, and suspends his functions and emoluments for a definite period of time, viz.: for a year, six months, or three months, from the date of the sentence, according to the culpability of the officer.

§ 141. *Reprimand, public or private.* A public reprimand is inflicted by the officer approving the sentence of the Court Martial, or by the Commanding officer of the regiment or garrison to which the party may belong, according to the terms of the sentence; and on which occasion the troops are paraded to hear it. The severity of the reprimand is not prescribed by the sentence, but is left to the discretion of the Commander-in-chief, by whose authority the sentence is put into execution, and it must be regulated according to circumstances and the degree of the offence. A private reprimand is given by the Commanding officer to the party without the presence of witnesses.

§ 142. The usual inferior punishment awarded against non-commissioned officers, is reduction; but, further penalties may be added according to the nature of the case. To sentence a non-commissioned officer merely to be reprimanded, is both unusual and inefficacious as a punishment. Such a sentence, therefore, ought never to be awarded by a Court Martial. The usual inferior punishments of a soldier are, imprisonment, solitary, or otherwise, hard labor and stoppage of pay.

§ 143. The Articles of War enact for certain offences, the reducing of non-commissioned officers to the station of private soldiers, as for the crimes of embezzling money, &c., or conniving at one soldier's having another to do such soldier's duty, &c. This power of reducing non-commissioned officers to the station of a private sentinel, rests, at all times, with the Commanding officer or Colonel of the regiment or corps, and can be exercised by his own authority, on a sufficient cause, without the intervention of a Court Martial; a discretionary power which has furnished a fruitful topic for discussion, and frequent occasion for blame, but which is founded on a just and necessary policy, and has never in practice been attended with evil consequences.

§ 144. In general, the sentence of Courts Martial declares the prisoner guilty, or not, of the special matters of his charge, and in the event of guilty, awards the proper punishment. But, sometimes the degree of criminality actually proved against the prisoner, though of the same nature, may fall short in extent of the crime or accusation; as, for example, the crime charged may be *desertion*, but the proof may amount to no more than *absence without leave*. In such case the Court, by its judgment, ought to acquit of the charge of desertion, but find the prisoner guilty of the inferior offence, and award a corresponding punishment. But although this rule ought to be followed where the offence proved is of the same nature, though less in degree, than the crime contained in the charge, it will not hold good, where the offence proved against the prisoner is either of a different nature altogether, from that which is charged, or of a higher degree of criminality; for the Court is not warranted to go beyond the charge, nor has the prisoner received a fair or legal notice to prepare his defence against either a different crime, or a crime of the same nature, but of a higher degree of guilt, than is contained in the charge. If, therefore, evidence should appear in the course of the trial, of greater criminality against the prisoner, than is contained in the charge, or of his guilt of a separate crime, it is competent for the Court, after exhausting the actual charges by its proper sentence, to report their opinion to the Commander, by whose order the Court is held, and to recommit the party to confinement, in order that he may be brought to a new trial.

§ 145. The form of the sentence of a Court Martial must vary according to the circumstances of the case on which it is pronounced, but a few general observations may here be made, applicable to all sentences whatever of General Courts Martial.

§ 146. As, according to the tenor of the oath administered to all the members of the Court, they are at no time whatsoever, nor upon any account, to discover or disclose the particular vote or opinion of any member, unless required to give evidence thereof in a Court of Justice, in a due course of law; [See Art. of War, 69,] it is evidently not proper that the sentence of the Court Martial should express by what majority of the members it was pronounced; because, that might lead to the discovery of the particular votes or opinions; nor, although the Court be unanimous in its judgment, is it proper to express that circumstance in the sentence, for this in fact is disclosing the votes and opinions of all the members. But in cases of capital punishment the law requiring the concurrence of two-thirds of the General Court Martial, the fact that two-thirds did concur must be stated; otherwise, the approving power could not be certain that that number did vote for the punishment. [See Art. of War, 87.]

§ 147. The opinions and sentence of the Court may be either general in their tenor, that is, declaring the prisoner guilty or not guilty of the articles of charge; or they may be special, finding certain parts proved, or not proved; in consequence of which it declared him guilty on those articles; for, in all cases the guilt or innocence of the prisoner, with respect to the particular charges, must be pointedly proved and declared; otherwise, the Court does not discharge the whole of its duty, which requires that it should not only decide whether the facts are proved or unproved, but likewise pronounce its judgment on the criminality of those facts.

§ 148. It was formerly a very usual custom, to express in the sentences of Courts Martial the particular Articles of War, of the breach of which the sentence declared the prisoner to be guilty; but, the more recent and better practice, is to omit all such reference to the Articles of War, as being in itself unnecessary, and frequently affording handle for cavilling and sophistical objections of irregularity, or incongruity with the articles referred to. If the sentence should be called in question, as not warranted by any positive Article of the Military Law, it is the province of the party, who thus arraigns the judgment, to point out that incongruity: for the presumption is, that the decrees and judgments of all Courts are warranted by law.

§ 149. For a reason nearly allied to the above, it would seem most advisable for Courts Martial in their opinions and sentences, to avoid all unnecessary minuteness in detailing and specifying the grounds of those opinions and judgments; and, in particular, to avoid all arguments in justification of their sentences;

for, it is unwise in any Court to hold forth to the public a challenge to impugn its judgment, or purposely to invite to a discussion of the grounds on which it has proceeded. If a sentence be general and without any assignment of special reasons, it may be defended by all good reasons which are applicable to the matter; but if it assign its special grounds, it must stand or fall by those grounds alone.

§ 150. It must at the same time be observed, that in cases of a circumstantial nature, and when the sentence of the Court is not general, upon the whole matters of charge, but special, finding the prisoner guilty of some points of accusation, and acquitting him of others; as the punishment to be awarded ought to be in strict proportion to the measure of guilt, so it may be extremely proper, in such cases to specify in the sentence, the particular grounds of the opinion and judgment of the Court.

RECOMMENDATION TO MERCY.

§ 151. If mitigating circumstances have appeared during the trial, though they may not enter into consideration in determining the sentence, they may afford adequate grounds for recommending the prisoner to mercy.

§ 152. No recommendation to mercy should be embraced in the body of the sentence, but it should be inserted after the signatures of the President and Judge Advocate. Those members only who recommend should sign the same.

REVISION.

§ 153. The authority by which a General Court Martial is convened, is competent to order a revision.

§ 154. Whenever the proceedings of a Court Martial are ordered to be revised, it is highly irregular and objectionable for the Court to call in and examine fresh witnesses. The revision is to be confined entirely to a reconsideration of the matter already recorded on the proceedings.

§ 155. A Court Martial, on revision, cannot alter or obliterate any part of the previous proceedings, or expunge from the record any testimony, however illegally it may have been admitted. Its duty in such case is, as the word revise indicates, to review and reconsider its judgment, opinion, and sentence. This obviously requires a reconsideration and weighing of the recorded testimony, with a view to correct, by an insertion of a second opinion, any error in the sentence, which may have arisen from inadvertency, misconception of law, or of the customs of service.

§ 156. It is to be particularly observed that, however excusable may be an adherence, from conscientious motives, to a finding and sentence once pronounced, yet, where error in judgment, arising from a misconception of the law, or of the custom of war in like cases, is brought to the notice of a Court Martial, supported by respectable authority, perseverance in error can be regarded in no other light, than as a dereliction of duty, improper in itself and unjust in its consequences.

CONFIRMATION, OR APPROVAL OR DISAPPROVAL OF THE SENTENCE.

§ 157. The sentence of a General Court Martial cannot be carried into execution, until after the whole of the proceedings shall have been laid before the officer ordering the same, or the officer commanding the troops, for the time being; neither can any sentence of a General Court Martial in time of peace, extending to the loss of life or the dismission of a Commissioned officer, or which shall, either in time of peace or war, respect a General Officer, be carried into execution, until after the whole proceedings shall have been transmitted to the Secretary of War, to be laid before the President of the United States, for his confirmation or disapproval, and orders in the case. All other sentences may be confirmed and executed by the officer ordering the Court to assemble, or the Commanding officer for the time being, as the case may be. [See Art. of War, 65.]

§ 158. When Courts Martial have on revision adhered to the judgment first pronounced, the opinion and sentence are sometimes confirmed, and not approved; the legal effect of which differs in no degree from approval.

§ 159. The opinion and sentence of a Court Martial may on other occasions be disapproved, and not confirmed; the effect of which is, to nullify the sentence; but not to the extent of exposing the prisoner to a second trial.

§ 160. Every officer authorized to order a General Court Martial, has power to pardon or mitigate any punishment ordered by such Court, except the sentence of death, or of cashiering an officer; which, in the cases where he has authority (as set forth by the 65th Art. of War,) to carry them into execution, he may suspend until the pleasure of the President of the United States be known; which suspension, together with copies of the proceedings of the Court Martial, the said officer will immediately transmit to the President for his determination. [See Art. of War, 89.]

§ 161. So that it appears that it is not in the power of any officer having authority to appoint General Courts Martial, to pardon, or mitigate the sentence of a General Court Martial, where the punishment is death, or the dismission of an officer. He must either cause the sentence to be carried into effect, or refer the matter to the Secretary of War, to be laid before the President for his decision in the case.

§ 162. Although it is lawful, as shown above, for the authority which orders the Court, to suspend, mitigate, or remit the sentence of a Court Martial, it does not authorize such authority to alter the nature of the punishment. This rule also applies to officers confirming the sentences of inferior Courts Martial. They may remit the whole, or any part of the sentence, but cannot, even with the consent of the party sentenced, commute or change the punishment.

§ 163. Mitigation, as the word implies, is to lessen or reduce in amount, or severity. Thus a soldier sentenced to receive fifty lashes, may have his punishment mitigated to twenty-five—and an officer sentenced to a year's suspension, may be suspended for only six months, or less, according to the circumstances attending his case. An officer sentenced to be dismissed the service, may have his punishment so mitigated by the President, as to be suspended for six months only, which is dismissing him for six months instead of a total dismissal. [See General Orders, No. 73, 17th Nov. 1829.]

§ 164. Courts Martial sometimes sentence culprits to solitary confinement, and without reflecting on its severity, extend it in certain cases to a year and even more. Long confinements of this character are dangerous to the health, and even tend to produce insanity. Officers having power to confirm such sentences, with much humanity, usually leave it discretionary with the Commanding officer of the regiment, or post where the punishment is to be inflicted, to continue or diminish the punishment according to the advice of the Medical Staff, in order to avoid such shocking consequences.

§ 165. The approval or confirmation of the Officer vested with the competent authority, is generally affixed with his signature to the proceedings, and a public notice of it usually announced in Orders.

EXECUTION OF THE SENTENCE.

---

§ 166. One of the great ends of punishment is the prevention of crime by example. Accordingly, Capital and Corporeal punishments, to be effectual and useful, are executed in the most public manner, as regards the troops. They are carried into effect in the presence of the Division, Brigade, Regiment, or Garrison, as the nature of the Court Martial and of the charge, and as the convenience of the service may dictate.

§ 167. In cases of Capital punishment by shooting, great ceremony is ordinarily observed; an execution party, consisting of ten or twelve men, commanded by a Sergeant, is usually ordered from the prisoner's regiment, and placed under the orders of a provost-marshal. The troops to witness the execution being formed on three sides of a square, the prisoner, escorted by a detachment, is brought on the ground. The provost-marshal heads the procession, followed by the band of the prisoner's regiment (drums muffled) playing the dead march in Saul, or some other appropriate air; the execution party comes next, then four men bearing on their shoulders the prisoner's coffin, which he himself follows, being sometimes attended by a chaplain; the escort brings up the rear. The procession passes down the front of the three faces of the square facing inwards; brigades or regiments being in line or in column, as their numbers and the nature of the ground may dictate. On the procession's arriving on the flank of each regiment, the band of that regiment plays the dead march in Saul, and continues till the procession has cleared its front. On arriving at the open face the music ceases; the prisoner is placed on the fatal spot marked by his coffin; the charge, sentence, and General Order or warrant for execution are read aloud; the chaplain, having engaged in prayer with the condemned, retires; the execution party forms at six or eight paces from the prisoner, and receives the word from the provost-marshal. If its fire should not prove instantaneously effectual, it is the duty of the provost-marshal, or some one selected for the purpose, to complete the sentence of the Court with his pistol. Sometimes the fire of a file or two is reserved to be prepared for this painful occurrence. After the execution the troops usually move past the body in slow time.

§ 168. Death by hanging is executed with less ceremony; the troops witnessing the execution being formed in square, on the gallows as a centre; the charge, sentence, and warrant or General Order, are read aloud, and an executioner, under the direction of the provost-marshal, performs his office.

§ 169. The usual manner of inflicting corporeal punishment is as follows: the brigade, garrison, regiment or detachment, being under arms, is formed in some retired spot, often in the ditch of an outwork of fortified places or forts, to receive the prisoner, who is brought by an escort to the centre; the brigade major or adjutant, as the case may be, proceeds to read aloud the charge, sometimes the proceedings, but invariably the sentence of the Court and the approval; the prisoner being uncovered and advanced a pace or two in front of the escort. The culprit is then directed to strip to the waist, and is tied to a stock of three muskets, so placed as to have their butts equidistant, and united firmly at the muzzles by means of lashing the bayonets. The culprit's hands are tied at the wrists, where the bayonets join, and his ancles to the small of the stock. At other times the prisoner is lashed to a gun wheel, and receives on his bare shoulders the lashes awarded, in succession, from the drummers or the trumpeters, till the punishment is completed or interrupted by order of the Commanding officer; the drum-major or trumpet-major counts each lash, or rather directs it, as the executioner does not give the lash till it is numbered; between each, a pause, equal to three paces in common time, takes place, which is marked by the executioner's encircling the cat round his head, or sometimes by taps of a drum.

§ 170. A Surgeon of the prisoner's regiment invariably superintends the punishment, and Staff-Surgeons also on general parades; should any symptoms arise, indicating the propriety of suspending the infliction, the Medical officer reports to the Senior officer on the parade, who directs accordingly. The Cat-o-nine-tails consists of a drum-stick, or handle of wood of equal length, having fixed to it nine ends of a whip-cord, about sixteen inches long, each knotted with three knots, one being near the end. The drum-major sees that the ends are not entangled during the infliction, so as to produce a more serious blow than intended, but that they are disengaged from time to time, and, if necessary, washed in water.

§ 171. Corporeal punishment by lashes, however, is never inflicted in the American Army, except for the crime of desertion. [See Act of Congress of 2d of March, 1823—Dec. 7.]

JUDGE ADVOCATE.

§ 172. For sustaining the interest of the United States, in trials before a General Court Martial, an officer is appointed under the title of Judge Advocate, to prosecute in their name; for, as in all criminal trials, the State, whose laws are violated, is understood to be the party injured, and entitled to demand redress by the punishment of the guilty person; so, in offences against the Military Law, which are not cognizable by the ordinary tribunals, but are declared to be specially so by Courts Martial, the Judge Advocate is appointed to prosecute, in the name of the United States, all officers and soldiers, who shall be accused of any breach of the Military Law, either as contained in the Articles of War, or other regulations issued for the government of the Army.

§ 173. The appropriate functions of the Judge Advocate, as an essential officer in all General Courts Martial, are various in their nature; and as the Articles of War do not describe them with much precision, it is proper to resort to the less positive, though equally binding authority, of established usage and practice.

§ 174. The Articles of War are silent on the subject of the Judge Advocate's assisting the Court with his counsels and advice as to any matters of form or law; it nevertheless is understood to be his duty to explain any doubts which may arise in the course of its deliberations, and to prevent any irregularities or deviations from the regular form of proceedings. For, it is to be observed, that in all matters touching the trials of crimes by Courts Martial, wherever the military law is silent, the rules of the common law, as generally recognized and enforced throughout the Union, must of necessity be resorted to.

§ 175. Though it is the duty of the Judge Advocate, as before observed, to prosecute in the name of the United States, yet he is so far to consider himself as counsel for the prisoner, after the prisoner shall have made his plea, as to object to any leading question to any of the witnesses, or any question to the prisoner, the answer to which might tend to criminate him. [See Art. of War, 69.]

§ 176. This duty is more especially incumbent on the Judge Advocate in cases where the prisoner has not the aid of professional counsel to direct him, which generally happens in the trials of private soldiers, who, having had few of the advantages of education, or opportunities for mental improvement, must stand greatly in need of advice under circumstances which are often sufficient to overwhelm the acutest intellect, and embarrass or suspend the powers of the most cultivated understanding. It is certainly not to be understood that, in discharging this office, which is prescribed solely by humanity, the Judge Advocate should, in the strictest sense, consider himself as bound to the duty of counsel, by exerting his ingenuity to defend the prisoner, at all hazards, against those charges which, in his capacity of prosecutor, he is, on the other hand, bound to urge, and sustain by proof; for, understood to this extent, the one duty is utterly inconsistent with the other. All that is required is, that in the same manner as, in civil courts of criminal jurisdiction, the judges are understood to be counsel for the person accused, the Judge Advocate in Courts Martial, shall do justice to the cause of the prisoner, by giving full weight to every circumstance or argument in his favor; shall bring the same fairly and completely into the view of the Court; shall suggest the supplying of all omissions in the leading of exculpatory evidence; shall engross in the written proceedings all matters which, either directly or by presumption, tend to the prisoner's defence; and finally, shall not avail himself of any advantage which superior knowledge or ability, or his influence with the Court may give him, in enforcing the conviction, rather than the acquittal, of the person accused.

§ 177. Many of the official functions of the Judge Advocate in trials before a General Court Martial, and in the matters preparatory and relative thereto, have been occasionally mentioned in the preceding chapters; but, for the sake of greater perspicuity, they will be here recapitulated in regular detail, likewise noticing such other particulars of the duty of this officer, as have not hitherto been mentioned.

§ 178. When a Court Martial is summoned by the proper authority, for the trial of any military offender, the Judge Advocate, being required to attend to his duty, and furnished with articles of charge or accusation, on which he is to prosecute, must, from the information of the accuser, instruct himself in all the circumstances of the case, and by what evidence the whole particulars are to be proved against the prisoner. Of these, it is proper that he should prepare, in writing, a short analysis, or plan, for his own regulation in the conduct of the trial, and examination of the witnesses. He ought then, if it has not been done by some other functionary, to give information to the prisoner of the time and place appointed for his trial, and furnish him, at the same time, with a copy of the charges that are to be exhibited against him, and likewise a correct detail of the members of the Court.

§ 179. The Judge Advocate ought then to hand in to the Adjutant-General, or Staff-officer charged with the details, a list of witnesses for the prosecution, in order that they may be summoned to give their attendance at the time and place appointed.

§ 180. It is proper, likewise, that he should desire the prisoner to make a similar application, to ensure the attendance of the witnesses necessary for his defence. These measures ought to be taken as early as possible, that there may be sufficient time for the arrival of witnesses who may be at a distance.

§ 181. When the Court is met for trial, and the members are regularly sworn, the Judge Advocate, after opening the prosecution by a recital of the charges, together with such detail of circumstances (if the case be circumstantial and complicated) as he may deem necessary, proceeds to examine his witnesses in support of the charges, while at the same time he acts as the recorder or clerk of the Court, in taking down the evidence in writing at full length, and as nearly as possible in the words of the witnesses.

§ 182. At the close of the business of each day, and in the interval before the next meeting of the Court, it is the duty of the Judge Advocate to make a fair copy of the proceedings; which he continues thus regularly to engross till the conclusion of the trial, when the whole is read over by him to the Court, before the members proceed to deliberate and form their opinions.

§ 183. The sentence of the Court must be fairly engrossed and subjoined to the record copy of the proceedings; and the whole must be authenticated by the signature of the President of the Court, and that of the Judge Advocate.

§ 184. It is required by the Articles of War, [See Art. 90.] that "every Judge Advocate, or person officiating as such, at any General Court Martial, shall transmit, with as much expedition as the opportunity of time and distance of place can admit, the original proceedings and sentence of such Court Martial, to the Secretary of War; which said original proceedings and sentence, shall be carefullly kept and preserved in the office of the said Secretary, to the end that the persons entitled thereto, may be enabled, upon application to the said office, to obtain copies thereof." The Judge Advocate sends the proceedings to the Secretary of War through the Adjutant-General.

REGIMENTAL AND GARRISON COURTS MARTIAL.

§ 185. The Articles of War provide that every officer commanding a regiment or corps, may appoint, for his own regiment or corps, Courts Martial to consist of three Commissioned officers for the trial and punishment of offences not capital, and decide upon their sentences. For the same purpose, all officers commanding any of the Garrisons, Forts, Barracks, or other places where the troops consist of different corps, may assemble Courts Martial, to consist of three Commissioned officers, and decide upon their sentences. [See Art. of War, 66.]

§ 186. The Articles of War contain no instruction or regulation with respect to the rank of these officers; but, the usual practice is to appoint a Captain and two subalterns, (if a Captain can be conveniently spared) and, in order that this duty may be equally shared, and all have the benefit of this school of instruction, it is customary in every regiment, for the Adjutant to keep a regular roster for this duty, as well as all other regimental duties.

§ 187. Regimental and Garrison Courts Martial, being only competent to the trial of lesser offences, or crimes which do not allow a capital punishment, and the cases that come before them not giving room for any intricacy of decision, or doubtful questions of law, have not the aid of a Judge Advocate to direct their proccedings. The President, therefore, as well as the other members, have on that account much responsibility; they ought to be particularly careful that their proceedings be strictly conformable to Military Law and the practice of the Army, as well as the great principles of justice and equity. The members of Regimental and Garrison Courts Martial take the same oaths as those of a General Court Martial, and the evidence is, in the same manner, given upon oath.

§ 188. The proceedings of Regimental and Garrison Courts Martial must be accurately taken down in writing, either by the President or by a member of the Court appointed by him, a duty generally devolved on the youngest member, and the sentence must be regularly signed by the President. No sentence of a Regimental or Garrison Court Martial can be put in execution, until it shall have been confirmed by the Commanding officer. [See Art. of War, 65.]

§ 189. For the redressing of all wrongs or injuries which an inferior officer or soldier may sustain from his superiors, the Articles of War declare, that "if any inferior officer or soldier shall think himself wronged by his Captain or other officer, he is to complain thereof to the Commanding officer of the regiment, who is thereby required to summon a Regimental Court Martial, for the doing justice to the complainant; from which Regimental Court Martial either party may, if he think himself still aggrieved, appeal to a General Court Martial." [See Art. of War, 35.] To check the frequency of ill-founded complaints, however, it is wisely enacted by the same article, that, "if upon a second hearing, the appeal shall appear vexatious and groundless, the person so appealing shall be punished at the discretion of the said Court Martial."

§ 190. It is material, however, to observe, that as no Commissioned officer is properly answerable to the judgment or sentence of a Regimental Court Martial, the Court on such complaint and inquiry can only pronounce its opinion, whether the complaint is well or ill founded; if it declare the latter, the complainant must either acquiesce in that opinion, or if he think himself still aggrieved, follow the mode of appeal to a General Court Martial, as above prescribed. If the Regimental Court Martial declare the complaint to be well founded, the complainant may, on that authority, request a General Court Martial to take cognizance of the injury, and bring the offender to proper punishment.

APPEAL FROM A REGIMENTAL TO A GENERAL COURT MARTIAL.

§ 191. The right of appeal from Regimental Courts Martial seems to be authorized in one particular case only, which is, when an inferior officer, (which here means non-commissioned officer) or soldier, shall think himself wronged by his Captain or other officer. In this case, if either party think himself still aggrieved, he may appeal to a General Court Martial.

§ 192. But if upon a second hearing the appeal shall appear vexatious and groundless, the person so appealing shall be punished at the discretion of the said Court Martial. It would hence appear, that in all such cases of alleged wrong or injustice, committed by superior officers towards their inferiors, the right of appeal cannot be refused; but must of course be granted, by the appointment of a General Court Martial, by the proper authority, to take cognizance of the case. The only check against rash and ill-founded applications in cases of the above nature, is the certainty that an adequate punishment will not fail to attend every unjust and groundless appeal. [See Art. of War, 35.]

§ 193. The wrongs here alluded to, have reference chiefly to matters of accounts between the Captain, or Commander of the company, and the soldier, relating to clothing and other supplies as well as to pay; and the Regimental Court, in examining into such transactions, may be considered more as a Court of Inquiry than a Court Martial; or, it may be viewed as an arbitration or board, called on to adjust and settle any differences arising in the settlements of accounts between the Captain and his men.

§ 194. One reason why a power of appeal is declared to be a matter of absolute right to inferior officers, or soldiers, complaining of being wronged by their officers, doubtless is, that a Regimental or Garrison Court Martial has not the power of inflicting any punishment on Commissioned officers. It can do no more than express its opinion, that the complaint is just, or the contrary, and where it is practicable and proper, relieve the sufferer as to any existing grievance; but, the injury complained of, however flagrant, must still have remained unredressed, as far as punishment is concerned, if an appeal to a General Court Martial had not been declared to be a matter of right to the party aggrieved.

COURTS OF INQUIRY.

---

§ 195. Courts of Inquiry are held by the same authority as General or Regimental Courts Martial, and have power to examine the witnesses on oath, and compel their attendance in the same manner. They are intrusted with power only "to examine into the nature of any transaction, accusation, or imputation against any officer or soldier." But they are not empowered to give their opinion on the merits of the case, excepting they shall be thereunto specially required. [See Art. of War, 91.] And, as Courts of Inquiry may be perverted to dishonorable purposes, and may be considered as engines of destruction to military merit, in the hands of weak and envious commandants, they are expressly prohibited, unless directed by the President of the United States, or demanded by the accused. [See Art. of War, 92.]

§ 196. Courts of Inquiry may consist of one or more officers, not exceeding three, and a Judge Advocate, or other suitable person, as a recorder, to reduce the proceedings and evidence to writing, all of whom must be sworn to the faithful performance of their duty. [See Art. of War, 92.]

§ 197. The Court may be ordered to report the *facts* of the case, with or without an opinion thereon. Such an order will not be complied with, by merely reporting the evidence or testimony; facts being the result, or conclusion established by weighing all the testimony, oral and documentary, before the Court.

§ 198. When a Court of Inquiry is directed to be assembled, the order should state whether the Court is to report the facts or not, and also whether or not it is to give an opinion on the merits. The Court should also be instructed, whether its attention is to be extended to a general investigation, or to be confined to the examination of particular points only, as the case may seem to require, in the judgment of the officer under whose authority it is assembled. Where the subject is multifarious, the Court should be instructed to state its opinion on each point separately, that the proper authority may be able to form his judgment.

§ 199. The Court may sit with open or closed doors, according to the nature of the transaction to be investigated. The Court generally sits with open doors; but, there may be delicate matters to be examined into, that might render it proper to sit with doors closed.

§ 200. The form of proceeding, in Courts of Inquiry, is nearly the same as that in Courts Martial: the members being assembled, and the parties interested called into Court, the Judge Advocate, or recorder, by direction of the President, reads the order by which the Court is constituted, and then administers to the members the following oath: "You shall well and truly examine and inquire, according to your evidence, into the matter now before you, without partiality, favor, affection, prejudice, or hope of reward: so help you God." [See Art. of War, 93.]

§ 201. The accusation is then read, and the witnesses are examined by the Court; and the parties accused are also permitted to cross-examine and interrogate the witnesses, so as to investigate fully the circumstances in question. [See Art. of War, 91.]

§ 202. The examination of witnesses being finished, the parties before the Court may address the Court, should they see fit to do so; after which the President orders the Court to be cleared. The recorder then reads over the whole of the proceedings, as well for the purpose of correcting the record, as for aiding the memory of the members of the Court. After mature deliberation on the evidence adduced, they proceed to find a state of facts, if so directed by the order constituting the Court, and to declare whether or not the grounds of accusation are sufficient to bring the matter before a General Court Martial; and also to give their opinion of the merits of the case, if so required.

§ 203. The Court should be careful to examine the order by which it is constituted, and be particular in conforming to the directions contained therein, either by giving a general opinion on the whole matter, a statement of facts only, or an opinion on such facts.

The proceedings of Courts of Inquiry have been returned to be reconsidered, when the Court has been unmindful of these points.

§ 204. It has been settled that a member of a Court of Inquiry may be objected to, for cause. [See proceedings of the Court of Inquiry, in the case of General E. P. Gaines, held at Frederick, Md., January 7th, 1837.]

§ 205. The proceedings must be authenticated by the signatures of the President and recorder, and delivered to the Commanding officer or authority which ordered the Court; and the said proceedings may be admitted in evidence by a Court Martial, in cases not capital, nor extending to the dismission of an officer, provided oral testimony cannot be obtained. [See Art. of War, 92.]

§ 206. Transactions may become the subject of investigation by Courts of Inquiry after the lapse of any number of years, on the application of the party accused, or by order of the President of the United States; the limitation mentioned in the 88th Article of War, being applicable only to General Courts Martial.

§ 207. It is not necessary to publish the proceedings or opinion of the Court, although it is usually done in General Orders.

§ 208. The Court is dissolved by the authority that ordered it to convene.

APPENDIX.

APPENDIX.

FORM No. 1.

Form of a General Order appointing a General Court Martial.

General Orders, No.	Head Quarters of the Army, Adjutant-General's Office. Washington, March 5th, 1838.

A General Court Martial, to consist of thirteen members, will convene at Fort Monroe, in the State of Virginia, on Monday the 2d of April, 18—, at 11 o'clock, A. M., or as soon thereafter as practicable, for the trial of Captain A. B., of the 1st Regiment of Artillery, and such other prisoners as may be brought before it.

The following Officers are detailed as members of the Court:

1. Colonel A. B.	1st Regiment of Artillery.
2. Colonel C. D.	3d Regiment of Infantry.
3. Lieut. Col. E. F.	1st Regiment of Dragoons.
4. Lieut. Col. F. G.	2d Regiment of Artillery.
5. Major W. T.	3d Regiment of Artillery.
6. Major N. M.	1st Regiment of Artillery.
7. Captain A. N.	3d Regiment of Infantry.

8.	Captain B. N.	1st Regiment of Artillery.
9.	Captain C. N.	2d Regiment of Infantry.
10.	Captain D. M.	3d Regiment of Artillery.
11.	Captain E. L.	1st Regiment of Infantry.
12.	Captain F. H.	1st Regiment of Artillery.
13.	Captain G. W.	1st Regiment of Artillery.

And the following Officers are detailed as supernumeraries:

Captain N. P.	2d Regiment of Infantry.
Captain D. B.	1st Regiment of Infantry.
Captain N. O.	1st Regiment of Artillery.

Captain S. R., of the 4th Regiment of Artillery, is hereby appointed Judge Advocate.

By order of A. M.

Major-General Commanding in Chief,

R. J.

Adjutant-General.

FORM No. 2.

General Orders, No.	Head Quarters of the Army, Adjutant-General's Office, Washington, April 9th, 1838.

A General Court Martial, to consist of as many members [within the prescribed limits] as can be assembled without manifest injury to the service, will convene at Fort Monroe, in the State of Virginia, on Tuesday the 23d of April, 18—, at 10 o'clock, A. M., or as soon thereafter as practicable, for the trial of Lieutenant C. D., of the 1st Regiment of Artillery, and such other prisoners as may be brought before it.

The Commanding officer, at Fort Monroe, will cause the members of the Court to be detailed from the officers of his command. First Lieutenant B. M., 2d Regiment of Artillery, is hereby appointed the Judge Advocate of the Court.

By order of A. M.

Major-General Commanding in Chief,

R. J.

Adjutant-General.

FORM No. 3.

Mode of recording the proceedings of a General, [or other] Court Martial.

Proceedings of a General Court Martial, held at Fort Monroe, in the State of Virginia, by virtue of the following Orders, viz:

[Here insert a copy of the Order convening the Court.]

Fort Monroe, Virginia,
Monday, April —, 183–.

The Court met pursuant to the above Orders.

PRESENT.

1. Colonel A. B. 1st Regt. of ———, *President.*

2. Colonel C. D.	*Members.*	3. Lieut. Col. E. F.
4. Lieut. Col. F. G.		5. Major W. T.
6. Major N. M.		7. Capt. A. N.
8. Capt. B. N.		9. Capt. C. N.
10. Capt. D. M.		11. Capt. E. L.
12. Capt. F. H.		13. Capt. W. G.

Captain S. R., Judge Advocate.

The court then proceeded to the trial of Captain A. B., of the ——— Regiment of ———, who being called into Court, and having heard the General Order read, was asked if he had any objection to any of the members named in the General Order, to which he replied in the negative.

The Court was then duly sworn, in his presence, and Captain A. B. was arraigned on the following charge and specifications, viz:

[Here insert the charge and specifications.]

To which the prisoner pleaded as follows:
Not Guilty, to the 1st specification,
Not Guilty, to the 2d specification,
Not Guilty, to the charge.

All persons required to give evidence were directed to withdraw, and remain in waiting until called for.

Lieut. A. B. of the 2d Regiment of Infantry, a witness for the prosecution, being duly sworn, says: that on the —— day of ——, &c. —— &c. ——.

Question by the Judge Advocate. —————— ?
Answer. ——————.
Question by the prisoner. —————— ?
Answer. ——————.
Question by the Court. —————— ?
Answer. ——————.

The prosecution was here closed, and the prisoner produced the following evidence:

Capt. C. D. of the Corps of ——, a witness for the defence, being duly sworn, says: that on the —— day of ——, &c. &c. ——.

Question by the prisoner. —————— ?
Answer. ——————.
Question by the Judge Advocate. —————— ?
Answer. ——————.
Question by the Court. —————— ?
Answer. ——————.

The prisoner having no further testimony to offer, requested to be indulged with —— days to prepare for his final defence.

The Court granted his request, and adjourned at o'clock, P. M., to meet again at —— o'clock, A. M., on Wednesday the —— day of ——.

SECOND DAY.

Wednesday, ——,183–.

The Court met pursuant to adjournment: present all the members.

The proceedings having been read over to the Court by the Judge Advocate, the prisoner, Captain A. B., made the following address in his defence:

[Here insert the defence, or if it be too long, it may be marked, and annexed.]

The Court then closed, and proceeded to deliberate on the testimony adduced, and pronounced the following

SENTENCE.

The Court, having maturely weighed and considered the evidence adduced in support of it, is of opinion that &c. —— &c. ——, and does therefore —— &c. —— &c.

A. B. Col. 1st Regt. of ——,
President.

S. R. Capt. —— Regt. of ——,
Judge Advocate.

FORM No. 4.

Form of an Order appointing a Garrison or Regimental Court Martial.

Orders, }
No. }

Head Quarters,
Fort Columbus, N. Y.
April 2d, 1838.

A Garrison, [or Regimental Court Martial,] to consist of Captain C. D. 1st Artillery, 1st Lieutenant D. F. 1st Artillery, and 2d Lieutenant G. H. 1st Artillery, will convene at the President's quarters to-morrow morning, at 11 o'clock, for the trial of Sergeant D. E. of ——— Company, ——— Regiment of Artillery, and such other prisoners as may be brought before it.

By order of Colonel A. B.
Commanding,
J. A.
Adjutant.

FORM No. 5.

Form of charges and specifications against a prisoner.

Charges and specifications preferred against Capt. C. D., of the 1st Regiment of Infantry.

CHARGE 1ST.

DISOBEDIENCE OF ORDERS.

Specification 1st. . . . In this, that he, the said Captain C. D., of the 1st Regiment of Infantry, being ordered, on the 30th day of September, 183–, at the Recruiting Depôt, in the Town of Newport, Kentucky, by Colonel A. B., of the 1st Regiment of Infantry, the Commanding officer of said Depôt, to take command of and march with a detachment of recruits to Jefferson Barracks, in the State of Missouri, did at said town of Newport, at the time aforesaid, refuse to take command of and march with said detachment of Recruits, thereby disobeying the lawful commands and orders of his superior and Commanding, officer, the said Colonel A. B.

Specification 2d. . . . In this, that he, the said Captain C. D., &c. &c.

E. F.
Major 1st Regiment of Infantry.

FORM No. 6.

Form of a General Order approving or disapproving the proceedings of a General Court Martial.

General Order, No. } Head Quarters of the Army,
Adjutant-General's Office.
Washington, January —, 183–.

I. . . At a General Court Martial which convened at ——— on the ——— of ———, 183–, pursuant to General Orders, No. —— of January 1830, and of which Brevet Brigadier-General ——— is President, was tried Captain —— of the —— Regiment of Artillery, on the following charges and specifications preferred by Major ——— of the —— Artillery, to wit:

CHARGE.

[Here insert charge. See Form No. 5.]

To which charge and specification the prisoner pleaded as follows:

To the 1st specification—[plea.]
To the 2nd specification—[plea.]
And guilty [or not guilty] to the charge.

FINDINGS AND SENTENCE.

The Court after mature deliberation on the testimony adduced, find the prisoner, Capt. ——— of ——— Regiment of Artillery, as follows:

Of the 1st specification—[finding.]
Of the 2nd specification—[finding.]
And guilty [or not guilty] of the charge.

And the Court do therefore sentence him, Captain ——, of —— Regiment of Artillery, to [here insert sentence.]

II. . . The proceedings, findings, and sentence are approved, [or disapproved,] &c. &c. &c.

(Here the authority which constituted the Court will add such remarks as he may think proper.)

III. . . The General Court Martial, of which Brevet Brigadier-General ——, is President, is hereby dissolved.

By order of A. M.
Major General, Commanding-in-chief,
R. S.
Adjutant-General.

ARTICLES OF WAR.

AN ACT FOR ESTABLISHING RULES AND ARTICLES FOR THE GOVERNMENT OF THE ARMIES OF THE UNITED STATES.

Section 1. *Be it enacted by the Senate and House of Representatives of the United States of America in Congress assembled,* That, from and after the passing of this act, the following shall be the Rules and Articles by which the Armies of the United States shall be governed:

Article 1. Every officer, now in the Army of the United States, shall, in six months after the passing of this act, and every officer who shall hereafter be appointed, shall, before he enters on the duties of his office, subscribe these rules and regulations.

Art. 2. It is earnestly recommended to all officers and soldiers diligently to attend Divine Service; and all officers who shall behave indecently or irreverently, at any place of Divine Worship, shall, if Commissioned officers, be brought before a General Court Martial, there to be publicly and severely reprimanded by the President; if non-commissioned officers or soldiers, every person so offending, shall, for his first offence, forfeit one-sixth of a dollar, to be deducted out of his next pay; for the second offence, he shall not only forfeit a like sum, but be confined twenty-four hours; and for every like offence, shall suffer and pay in like manner; which money so forfeited, shall be applied by the Captain or senior officer of the troop or company, to the use of the sick soldiers of the company or troop to which the offender belongs.

Art. 3. Any non-commissioned officer or soldier who shall use any profane oath or execration, shall incur the penalties expressed in the foregoing article; and a Commissioned officer shall forfeit and pay for each and every such offence, one dollar, to be applied as in the preceding article.

Art. 4. Every Chaplain commissioned in the Army or Armies of the United States, who shall absent himself from the duties assigned him, (excepting in cases of sickness or leave of absence,) shall, on conviction thereof before a Court Martial, be fined not exceeding one month's pay, besides the loss of his pay during his absence; or be discharged, as the said Court Martial shall judge proper.

Art. 5. Any officer or soldier who shall use contemptuous or disrespectful words against the President of the United States, against the Vice President thereof, against the Congress of the United States, or against the Chief Magistrate or Legislature of any of the United States, in which he may be quartered, if a Commissioned officer, shall be cashiered, or otherwise punished, as a Court Martial shall direct; if a non-commissioned officer or soldier, he shall suffer such punishment as shall be inflicted on him by the sentence of a Court Martial.

Art. 6. Any officer or soldier who shall behave himself with contempt or disrespect towards his Commanding officer, shall be punished according to the nature of his offence, by the judgment of a Court Martial.

Art. 7. Any officer or soldier who shall begin, excite, cause, or join, in any mutiny, or sedition, in any troop or company in the service of the United States, or in any party, post, detachment, or guard, shall suffer death, or such other punishment as by a Court Martial shall be inflicted.

ART. 8. Any officer, non-commissioned officer, or soldier, who, being present at any mutiny or sedition, does not use his utmost endeavor to suppress the same, or coming to the know ledge of any intended mutiny, does not without delay, give information thereof to his Commanding officer, shall be punished by the sentence of a Court Martial with death, or otherwise, according to the nature of his offence.

ART. 9. Any officer or soldier who shall strike his superior officer, or draw or lift up any weapon, to offer any violence against him, being in the execution of his office, on any pretence whatsoever, or shall disobey any lawful command of his superior officer, shall suffer death, or such other punishment as shall, according to the nature of his offence, be inflicted upon him by the sentence of a Court Martial.

ART. 10. Every non-commissioned officer or soldier, who shall enlist himself in the service of the United States, shall, at the time of enlisting himself, or within six days afterwards, have the Articles for the government of the Armies of the United States, read to him, and shall, by the officer who enlisted him, or by the Commanding officer of the troop or company into which he was enlisted, be taken before the next justice of the peace, or chief magistrate of any city or town corporate, not being an officer of the Army, or where recourse cannot be had to the civil magistrate, before the Judge Advocate, and in his presence, shall take the following oath or affirmation: "I, A B, do solemnly swear or affirm, (as the case may be,) that I will bear true allegiance to the United States of America, and that I will serve them honestly and faithfully against all their enemies or opposers whatsoever; and observe and obey the orders of the President of the United States, and the orders of the officers appointed over me, according to the Rules and Articles for the government of the Armies of the United States." Which justice, magistrate, or Judge Advocate, is to give the officer a certificate, signifying that the man enlisted, did take the said oath or affirmation.

ART. 11. After a non-commissioned officer or soldier shall have been duly enlisted and sworn, he shall not be dismissed the service, without a discharge in writing; and no discharge granted to him shall be sufficient, which is not signed by a field officer of the regiment to which he belongs, or Commanding officer, where no field officer of the regiment is present; and no discharge shall be given to a non-commissioned officer or soldier, before his term of service has expired, but by order of the President, the Secretary of War, the Commanding officer of a department, or the sentence of a General Court Martial; nor shall a Commissioned officer be discharged the service, but by order of the President of the United States, or by sentence of a General Court Martial.

ART. 12. Every Colonel or other officer commanding a regiment, troop, or company, and actually quartered with it, may give furloughs to non-commissioned officers or soldiers, in such numbers, and for so long a time, as he shall judge to be most consistent with the good of the service; and a Captain, or other inferior officer, commanding a troop or company, or in any garrison, fort, or barrack, of the United States, (his field officer being absent,) may give furloughs to non-commissioned officers or soldiers, for a time not exceeding twenty days in six months, but not to more than two persons to be absent at the same time, excepting some extraordinary occasion should require it.

ART. 13. At every muster, the Commanding officer of each regiment, troop, or company, there present, shall give to the Commissary of Musters, or other officer who musters the said regiment, troop, or company, certificates signed by himself, signifying how long such officers as shall not appear at the said muster, have been absent, and the reason of their absence. In like manner, the Commanding officer of every troop or company, shall give certificates, signifying the reasons of the absence of the non-commissioned officers and private soldiers; which reasons, and time of absence, shall be inserted in the muster rolls, opposite the names of the respective absent officers and soldiers. The certificates shall, together with the muster rolls, be remitted by the Commissary of Musters, or other officer mustering, to the Department of War, as speedily as the distance of the place will admit.

Art. 14. Every officer who shall be convicted before a General Court Martial, of having signed a false certificate, relating to the absence of either officer or private soldier, or relative to his or their pay, shall be cashiered.

Art. 15. Every officer who shall knowingly make a false muster of man or horse, and every officer or Commissary of Musters, who shall willingly sign, direct, or allow the signing of muster rolls, wherein such false muster is contained, shall, upon proof made thereof, by two witnesses before a General Court Martial, be cashiered, and shall be thereby utterly disabled to have or hold any office or employment in the service of the United States.

Art. 16. Any Commissary of Musters, or other officer, who shall be convicted of having taken money, or other thing, by way of gratification, on mustering any regiment, troop, or company, or on signing muster rolls, shall be displaced from his office, and shall be thereby utterly disabled to have or hold any office or employment in the service of the United States.

Art. 17. Any officer who shall presume to muster a person as a soldier, who is not a soldier, shall be deemed guilty of having made a false muster, and shall suffer accordingly.

Art. 18. Every officer who shall knowingly make a false return to the Department of War, or to any of his superior officers, authorized to call for such returns, of the state of the regiment, troop, or company, or garrison, under his command, or of the arms, ammunition, clothing, or other stores thereunto belonging, shall, on conviction thereof before a Court Martial, be cashiered.

Art. 19. The Commanding officer of every regiment, troop, or independent company, or garrison, of the United

States, shall, in the beginning of every month, remit, through the proper channels, to the Department of War, an exact return of the regiment, troop, independent company, or garrison, under his command, specifying the names of the officers then absent from their posts, with the reasons for and the time of their absence. And any officer who shall be convicted of having, through neglect or design, omitted sending such returns, shall be punished according to the nature of his crime, by the judgment of a General Court Martial.

Art. 20. All officers and soldiers who have received pay, or have been duly enlisted in the service of the United States, and shall be convicted of having deserted the same, shall suffer death, or such other punishment as by sentence of a Court Martial shall be inflicted.

Art. 21. Any non-commissioned officer or soldier who shall, without leave from his commanding officer, absent himself from his troop, company, or detachment, shall, upon being convicted thereof, be punished according to the nature of his offence, at the discretion of a Court Martial.

Art. 22. No non-commissioned officer or soldier shall enlist himself in any other regiment, troop, or company, without a regular discharge from the regiment, troop, or company, in which he last served, on the penalty of being reputed a deserter, and suffering accordingly. And in case any officer shall knowingly receive and entertain such non-commissioned officer or soldier, or shall not, after his being discovered to be a deserter, immediately confine him, and give notice thereof to the corps in which he last served, the said officer shall, by a Court Martial, be cashiered.

Art. 23. Any officer or soldier who shall be convicted of having advised or persuaded any other officer or soldier to desert the service of the United States, shall suffer death or such other punishment as shall be inflicted upon him by the sentence of a Court Martial.

Art. 24. No officer or soldier shall use any reproachful or

provoking speeches or gestures to another, upon pain, if an officer, of being put in arrest; if a soldier, confined, and of asking pardon of the party offended, in the presence of his Commanding officer.

ART. 25. No officer or soldier shall send a challenge to another officer or soldier, to fight a duel, or accept a challenge if sent, upon pain, if a Commissioned officer, of being cashiered; if a non-commissioned officer or soldier, of suffering corporeal punishment, at the discretion of a Court Martial.

ART. 26. If any Commissioned or non-commissioned officer commanding a guard, shall knowingly or willingly suffer any person whatsoever to go forth to fight a duel, he shall be punished as a challenger; and all seconds, promoters, and carriers of challenges, in order to duels, shall be deemed principals, and punished accordingly. And it shall be the duty of every officer commanding an army, regiment, company, post, or detachment, who is knowing to a challenge being given or accepted by any officer, non-commissioned officer or soldier, under his command, or has reason to believe the same to be the case, immediately to arrest and bring to trial such offenders.

ART. 27. All officers, of what condition soever, have power to part and quell all quarrels, frays, and disorders, though the persons concerned should belong to another regiment, troop, or company; and either to order officers into arrest, or non-commissioned officers or soldiers into confinement, until their proper superior officers shall be acquainted therewith; and whosoever shall refuse to obey such officer, (though of an inferior rank,) or shall draw his sword upon him, shall be punished at the discretion of a General Court Martial.

ART. 28. Any officer or soldier who shall upbraid another for refusing a challenge, shall himself be punished as a challenger; and all officers and soldiers are hereby discharged from any disgrace or opinion of disadvantage which might arise from their having refused to accept of challenges, as they will only have acted in obedience to the laws, and done their duty as good soldiers who subject themselves to discipline.

ART. 29. No sutler shall be permitted to sell any kind of liquor or victuals, or to keep their houses or shops open for the entertainment of soldiers, after nine at night, or before the beating of the reveilles, or upon Sundays, during Divine service or sermon, on the penalty of being dismissed from all future sutling.

ART. 30. All officers commanding in the field, forts, barracks, or garrisons, of the United States, are hereby required to see that the persons permitted to suttle shall supply the soldiers with good and wholesome provisions, or other articles, at a reasonable price, as they shall be answerable for their neglect.

ART. 31. No officer commanding in any of the garrisons, forts, or barracks, of the United States, shall exact exorbitant prices for houses or stalls, let out to sutlers, or connive at the like exactions in others; nor by his own authority, and for his private advantage, lay any duty or imposition upon, or be interested in, the sale of any victuals, liquors, or other necessaries of life brought into the garrison, fort, or barracks, for the use of the soldiers, on the penalty of being discharged from the service.

ART. 32. Every officer commanding in quarters, garrisons, or on the march, shall keep good order, and, to the utmost of his power, redress all abuses or disorders which may be committed by any officer or soldier under his command; if, upon complaint made to him of officers or soldiers beating or otherwise ill-treating any person, of disturbing fairs or markets, or of committing any kinds of riots, to the disquieting of the citizens of the United States, he, the said commander, who shall refuse or omit to see justice done to the offender or offenders, and reparation made to the party or parties injured, as far as part of the offender's pay shall enable him or them, shall, upon proof thereof, be cashiered, or otherwise punished, as a General Court Martial shall direct.

ART. 33. When any Commissioned officer or soldier shall be accused of a capital crime, or of having used violence, or committed any offence against the person or property of any citizen of any of the United States, such as is punishable by the known laws of the land, the Commanding officer and officers of every regiment, troop, or company to which the person or persons so accused shall belong, are hereby required, upon application duly made by, or in behalf of the party or parties injured, to use their utmost endeavors to deliver over such accused person or persons to the civil magistrate, and likewise to be aiding and assisting to the officers of justice in apprehending and securing the person or persons so accused, in order to bring him or them to trial. If any Commanding officer or officers shall wilfully neglect or shall refuse, upon the application aforesaid, to deliver over such accused person or persons to the civil magistrates, or to be aiding and assisting to the officers of justice in apprehending such person or persons, the officer or officers so offending shall be cashiered.

ART. 34. If any officer shall think himself wronged by his Colonel, or the Commanding officer of the regiment, and shall, upon due application being made to him, be refused redress, he may complain to the General commanding in the State or Territory where such regiment shall be stationed, in order to obtain justice; who is hereby required to examine into the said complaint, and take proper measures for redressing the wrong complained of, and transmit, as soon as possible, to the Department of War, a true state of such complaint, with the proceedings had thereon.

ART. 35. If any inferior officer or soldier, shall think himself wronged by his Captain, or other officer, he is to complain thereof to the Commanding officer of the regiment, who is hereby required to summon a Regimental Court Martial, for the doing justice to the complainant; from which Regimental

Court Martial either party may, if he thinks himself still aggrieved, appeal to a General Court Martial. But if, upon a second hearing, the appeal shall appear vexatious and groundless, the person so appealing, shall be punished at the discretion of the said Court Martial.

Art. 36. Any commissioned officer, storekeeper, or commissary, who shall be convicted at a General Court Martial, of having sold, without a proper order for that purpose, embezzled, misapplied, or wilfully, or through neglect, suffered any of the provisions, forage, arms, clothing, ammunition, or other military stores, belonging to the United States, to be spoiled or damaged, shall, at his own expense, make good the loss or damages, and shall, moreover, forfeit all his pay, and be dismissed from the service.

Art. 37. Any non-commissioned officer or soldier who shall be convicted at a Regimental Court Martial, of having sold, or designedly, or through neglect, wasted the ammunition delivered out to him, to be employed in the service of the United States, shall be punished at the discretion of such Court.

Art. 38. Every non-commissioned officer or soldier who shall be convicted before a Court Martial, of having sold, lost, or spoiled, through neglect, his horse, arms, clothes, or accoutrements, shall undergo such weekly stoppages (not exceeding the half of his pay,) as such Court Martial shall judge sufficient, for repairing the loss or damage; and shall suffer confinement, or such other corporeal punishment as his crime shall deserve.

Art. 39. Every officer who shall be convicted before a Court Martial, of having embezzled, or misapplied, any money with which he may have been entrusted, for the payment of the men under his command, or for enlisting men into the service, or for other purposes, if a Commissioned officer, shall be cashiered, and compelled to refund the money; if a non-commissioned officer, shall be reduced to the ranks, be put under stoppages, until the money be made good, and suffer such corporeal punishment as such Court Martial shall direct.

Art. 40. Every Captain of a troop, or company, is charged with the arms, accoutrements, ammunition, clothing, or other warlike stores, belonging to the troop or company under his command, which he is to be accountable for to his Colonel, in case of their being lost, spoiled, or damaged, not by unavoidable accidents, or on actual service.

Art. 41. All non-commissioned officers and soldiers who shall be found one mile from the camp, without leave in writing, from their Commanding officer, shall suffer such punishment as shall be inflicted upon them by the sentence of a Court Martial.

Art. 42. No officer or soldier shall lie out of his quarters, garrison, or camp, without leave from his superior officer, upon penalty of being punished according to the nature of his offence, by the sentence of a Court Martial.

Art. 43. Every non-commissioned officer and soldier shall retire to his quarters or tent, at the beating of the retreat; in default of which he shall be punished according to the nature of his offence.

Art. 44. No officer, non-commissioned officer, or soldier, shall fail in repairing, at the time fixed, to the place of parade, of exercise, or other rendezvous, appointed by his Commanding officer, if not prevented by sickness, or some other evident necessity; or shall go from the said place of rendezvous, without leave from his Commanding officer, before he shall be regularly dismissed or relieved, on the penalty of being punished according to the nature of his offence, by the sentence of a Court Martial.

Art. 45. Any Commissioned officer who shall be found drunk on his guard, party, or other duty, shall be cashiered. Any non-commissioned officer or soldier so offending, shall suffer such corporeal punishment as shall be inflicted by the sentence of a Court Martial.

Art. 46. Any sentinel who shall be found sleeping upon his post, or shall leave it before he shall be regularly relieved, shall suffer death, or such other punishment as shall be inflicted by the sentence of a Court Martial.

Art. 47. No soldier belonging to any regiment, troop, or company, shall hire another to do his duty for him, or be excused from duty, but in case of sickness, disability, or leave of absence; and every such soldier found guilty of hiring his duty, as also the party so hired to do another's duty, shall be punished at the discretion of a Regimental Court Martial.

Art. 48. And every non-commissioned officer conniving at such hiring of duty aforesaid, shall be reduced; and every Commissioned officer, knowing and allowing such ill practices in the service, shall be punished by the judgment of a General Court Martial.

Art. 49. Any officer belonging to the service of the United States, who, by discharging of fire-arms, drawing of swords, beating of drums, or by any other means whatsoever, shall occasion false alarms, in camp, garrison, or quarters, shall suffer death, or such other punishment as shall be ordered by the sentence of a General Court Martial.

Art. 50. Any officer or soldier, who shall, without urgent necessity, or without the leave of his superior officer, quit his guard, platoon, or division, shall be punished according to the nature of his offence, by the sentence of a Court Martial.

Art. 51. No officer or soldier shall do violence to any person who brings provisions or other necessaries to the camp, garrison, or quarters, of the forces of the United States, employed in any parts out of the said States, upon pain of death, or such other punishment as a Court Martial shall direct.

Art. 52. Any officer or soldier who shall misbehave himself before the enemy, run away, or shamefully abandon any fort, post, or guard, which he or they may be commanded to defend, or speak words inducing others to do the like; or shall cast away his arms and ammunition, or who shall quit his post or colors to plunder and pillage; every such offender, being duly convicted thereof, shall suffer death, or such other punishment as shall be ordered by the sentence of a General Court Martial.

Art. 53. Any person belonging to the Armies of the United States, who shall make known the watchword to any person who is not entitled to receive it according to the rules and discipline of war, or shall presume to give a parole or watchword different from what he received, shall suffer death, or such other punishment as shall be ordered by the sentence of a General Court Martial.

Art. 54. All officers and soldiers are to behave themselves orderly in quarters and on their march; and whosoever shall commit any waste or spoil, either in walks of trees, parks, warrens, fish-ponds, houses, or gardens, cornfields, enclosures of meadows, or shall maliciously destroy any property whatsoever belonging to the inhabitants of the United States, unless by order of the then Commander-in-chief of the Armies of the said States, shall, (besides such penalties as they are liable to by law,) be punished according to the nature and degree of the offence, by the judgment of a Regimental or General Court Martial.

Art. 55. Whosoever, belonging to the Armies of the United States employed in foreign parts, shall force a safe guard, shall suffer death.

Art. 56. Whosoever shall relieve the enemy with money, victuals, or ammunition, or shall knowingly harbor or protect an enemy, shall suffer death, or such other punishment as shall be ordered by the sentence of a Court Martial.

Art. 57. Whosoever shall be convicted of holding correspondence with, or giving intelligence to the enemy, either directly or indirectly, shall suffer death, or such other punishment as shall be ordered by the sentence of a Court Martial.

Art. 58. All public stores taken in the enemy's camp, towns, forts, or magazines, whether of artillery, ammunition, clothing, forage, or provisions, shall be secured for the service of the United States; for the neglect of which the Commanding officer is to be answerable.

Art. 59. If any Commander of any garrison, fortress, or post, shall be compelled by the officers and soldiers under his command, to give up to the enemy, or to abandon it, the Commissioned officers, non-commissioned officers, or soldiers, who shall be convicted of having so offended, shall suffer death, or such other punishment as shall be inflicted upon them by the sentence of a Court Martial.

Art. 60. All sutlers or retainers to the camp, and all persons whatsoever, serving with the Armies of the United States in the field, though not enlisted soldiers, are to be subject to orders, according to the rules and discipline of war.

Art. 61. Officers having brevets, or commissions of a prior date to those of the regiment in which they serve, may take place in Courts Martial and on detachments, when composed of different corps, according to the ranks given them in their brevets or dates of their former commissions; but in the regiment, troop, or company, to which such officers belong, they shall do duty and take rank both in Courts Martial and on detachments which shall be composed only of their own corps, according to the commissions by which they are mustered in the said corps.

Art. 62. If, upon marches, guards, or in quarters, different corps of the Army shall happen to join, or do duty together, the officer highest in rank of the line of the Army, Marine Corps, or Militia, by commission, there on duty or in quarters, shall command the whole, and give orders for what is needful to the service, unless otherwise specially directed by the President of the United States, according to the nature of the case.

Art. 63. The functions of the engineers being generally confined to the most elevated branch of military science, they are not to assume, nor are they subject to be ordered on any duty beyond the line of their immediate profession, except by the special order of the President of the United States; but they are to receive every mark of respect to which their rank in the Army may entitle them respectively, and are liable to be transferred at the discretion of the President, from one corps to another, regard being paid to rank.

Art. 64. General Courts Martial may consist of any number of Commissioned officers, from five to thirteen, inclusively; but they shall not consist of less than thirteen, where that number can be convened without manifest injury to the service.

Art. 65. Any general officer commanding an Army, or Colonel commanding a separate department, may appoint General Courts Martial whenever necessary. But no sentence of a Court Martial shall be carried into execution until after the whole proceedings shall have been laid before the officer ordering the same, or the officer commanding the troops for the time being, neither shall any sentence of a General Court Martial, in time of peace, extending to the loss of life, or the dismission of a Commissioned officer, or which shall, either in time of peace or war, respect a general officer, be carried into execution, until after the whole proceedings shall have been transmitted to the Secretary of War, to be laid before the President of the United States, for his confirmation or disapproval, and orders in the case. All other sentences may be confirmed and executed by the officer ordering the Court to assemble, or the Commanding officer for the time being, as the case may be.

Art. 66. Every officer commanding a regiment or corps, may appoint, for his own regiment or corps, Courts Martial, to consist of three Commissioned officers, for the trial and punishment of offences not capital, and decide upon their sentences. For the same purpose, all officers commanding any of the garrisons, forts, barracks, or other places where the troops consist of different corps, may assemble Courts Martial, to consist of three Commissioned officers, and decide upon their sentences.

Art. 67. No Garrison or Regimental Court Martial shall have the power to try capital cases, or Commissioned officers, neither shall they inflict a fine exceeding one month's pay, nor imprison, nor put to hard labor, any non-commissioned officer or soldier, for a longer time than one month.

ART. 68. Whenever it may be found convenient and necessary to the public service, the officers of the marines shall be associated with the officers of the land forces, for the purpose of holding Courts Martial and trying offenders belonging to either; and in such cases, the orders of the senior officer of either corps, who may be present, and duly authorized, shall be received and obeyed.

ART. 69. The Judge Advocate, or some person deputed by him or by the General, or officer commanding the Army, detachment, or garrison, shall prosecute in the name of the United States, but shall so far consider himself as counsel for the prisoner, after the said prisoner shall have made his plea, as to object to any leading question to any of the witnesses, or any question to the prisoner, the answer to which might tend to criminate himself; and administer to each member of the Court, before they proceed upon any trial, the following oath, which shall also be taken by all members of the Regimental and Garrison Courts Martial:

"You, A B, do swear, that you will well and truly try and determine, according to evidence, the matter now before you, between the United States of America and the prisoner to be tried, and that you will duly administer justice, according to the provisions of 'An act establishing Rules and Articles for the government of the Armies of the United States,' without partiality, favor, or affection; and if any doubt shall arise, not explained by said Articles, according to your conscience, the best of your understanding, and the custom of war in like cases; and you do further swear, that you will not divulge the sentence of the Court until it shall be published by the proper authority; neither will you disclose or discover the vote or opinion of any particular member of the Court Martial, unless required to give evidence thereof, as a witness, by a court of justice, in a due course of law. So help you God."

And as soon as the said oath shall have been administered to the respective members, the President of the Court shall administer to the Judge Advocate, or person officiating as such, an oath in the following words :

"You, A B, do swear, that you will not disclose or discover the vote or opinion of any particular member of the Court Martial, unless required to give evidence thereof, as a witness, by a court of justice, in due course of law; nor divulge the sentence of the court to any but the proper authority, until it shall be duly disclosed by the same. So help you God."

Art. 70. When a prisoner, arraigned before a General Court Martial, shall, from obstinacy and deliberate design, stand mute, or answer foreign to the purpose, the Court may proceed to trial and judgment, as if the prisoner had regularly pleaded not guilty.

Art. 71. When a member shall be challenged by a prisoner, he must state his cause of challenge, of which the Court shall, after due deliberation, determine the relevancy or validity, and decide accordingly; and no challenge to more than one member at a time, shall be received by the Court.

Art. 72. All the members of a Court Martial are to behave with decency and calmness; and in giving their votes, are to begin with the youngest in commission.

Art. 73. All persons who give evidence before a Court Martial, are to be examined on oath or affirmation, in the following form :

"You swear, or affirm, (as the case may be,) the evidence you shall give in the cause now in hearing, shall be the truth, the whole truth, and nothing but the truth. So help you God."

Art. 74. On the trials of cases not capital, before Courts Martial, the deposition of witnesses, not in the line or staff of the Army, may be taken before some justice of the peace, and read in evidence; provided the prosecutor and person accused are present at the taking the same, or are duly notified thereof.

ART. 75. No officer shall be tried but by a General Court Martial, nor by officers of an inferior rank, if it can be avoided. Nor shall any proceedings or trials be carried on, excepting between the hours of eight in the morning, and three in the afternoon, excepting in cases which, in the opinion of the officer appointing the Court Martial, require immediate attention.

ART. 76. No person whatsoever shall use any menacing words, signs, or gestures, in presence of a Court Martial, or shall cause any disorder or riot, or disturb their proceedings, on the penalty of being punished, at the discretion of the said Court Martial.

ART. 77. Whenever any officer shall be charged with a crime, he shall be arrested and confined in his barracks, quarters, or tent, and deprived of his sword, by the Commanding officer. And any officer who shall leave his confinement before he shall be set at liberty by his Commanding officer, or by a superior officer, shall be cashiered.

ART. 78. Non-commissioned officers and soldiers, charged with crimes, shall be confined until tried by a Court Martial, or released by proper authority.

ART. 79. No officer or soldier who shall be put in arrest, shall continue in confinement more than eight days, or until such time as a Court Martial can be assembled.

ART. 80. No officer commanding a guard, or provost-marshal, shall refuse to receive or keep any prisoner committed to his charge by an officer belonging to the forces of the United States; provided the officer committing shall, at the same time, deliver an account in writing, signed by himself, of the crime with which the said prisoner is charged.

ART. 81. No officer commanding a guard, or provost-marshal, shall presume to release any person committed to his charge, without proper authority for so doing, nor shall he suffer any person to escape, on the penalty of being punished for it by the sentence of a Court Martial.

Art. 82. Every officer or provost-marshal, to whose charge prisoners shall be committed, shall, within twenty-four hours after such commitment, or as soon as he shall be relieved from his guard, make report in writing, to the Commanding officer, of their names, their crimes, and the names of the officers who committed them, on the penalty of being punished for disobedience or neglect, at the discretion of a Court Martial.

Art. 83. Any Commissioned officer, convicted before a General Court Martial of conduct unbecoming an officer and a gentleman, shall be dismissed the service.

Art. 84. In cases where a Court Martial may think it proper to sentence a Commissioned officer to be suspended from command, they shall have power also to suspend his pay and emoluments for the same time, according to the nature and heinousness of the offence.

Art. 85. In all cases where a Commissioned officer is cashiered for cowardice or fraud, it shall be added in the sentence, that the crime, name, and place of abode, and punishment of the delinquent, be published in the newspapers, in and about the camp, and of the particular State from which the offender came, or where he usually resides, after which it shall be deemed scandalous for an officer to associate with him.

Art. 86. The Commanding officer of any post or detachment, in which there shall not be a number of officers adequate to form a General Court Martial, shall, in cases which require the cognizance of such a Court, report to the Commanding officer of the department, who shall order a Court to be assembled at the nearest post or detachment, and the party accused, with necessary witnesses, to be transported to the place where the said Court Martial shall be assembled.

Art. 87. No person shall be sentenced to suffer death, but by the concurrence of two thirds of the members of a General

Court Martial, nor except in the cases herein expressly mentioned; *nor shall more than fifty lashes be inflicted on any offender, at the discretion of a Court Martial*;* and no officer, non-commissioned officer, soldier, or follower of the Army, shall be tried a second time for the same offence.

Art. 88. No person shall be liable to be tried and punished by a General Court Martial for any offence which shall appear to have been committed more than two years before the issuing of the order for such trial, unless the person, by reason of having absented himself, or some other manifest impediment, shall not have been amenable to justice within that period.

Art. 89. Every officer authorized to order a General Court Martial, shall have power to pardon or mitigate any punishment ordered by such Court, except the sentence of death, or of cashiering an officer; which, in the cases where he has authority (by Article 65) to carry them into execution, he may suspend, until the pleasure of the President of the United States can be known; which suspension, together with copies of the proceedings of the Court Martial, the said officer shall immediately transmit to the President for his determination. And the Colonel or Commanding officer of the regiment or garrison, where any Regimental or Garrison Court Martial shall be held, may pardon or mitigate any punishment ordered by such court to be inflicted.

Art. 90. Every Judge Advocate, or person officiating as such, at any General Court Martial, shall transmit, with as much expedition as the opportunity of time and distance of place can admit, the original proceedings and sentence of such Court Martial, to the Secretary of War; which said original proceedings and sentence shall be carefully kept and preserved in the office of said Secretary, to the end that the persons entitled thereto may be enabled, upon application to the said office, to obtain copies thereof.

* Punishment by stripes or lashes abolished. See paragraph 3, page 135.

The party tried by any General Court Martial, shall, upon demand thereof, made by himself, or by any person or persons in his behalf, be entitled to a copy of the sentence and proceedings of such Court Martial.

Art. 91. In cases where the General or Commanding officer may order a Court of Inquiry to examine into the nature of any transaction, accusation, or imputation, against any officer or soldier, the said Court shall consist of one or more officers, not exceeding three, and a Judge Advocate, or other suitable person, as a recorder, to reduce the proceedings and evidence to writing, all of whom shall be sworn to the faithful performance of their duty. This Court shall have the same power to summon witnesses as a Court Martial, and to examine them on oath. But they shall not give their opinion on the merits of the case, excepting they shall be thereto specially required. The parties accused shall also be permitted to cross-examine and interrogate the witnesses, so as to investigate fully the circumstances in the question.

Art. 92. The proceedings of a Court of Inquiry, must be authenticated by the signature of the recorder and the President, and delivered to the Commanding officer, and the said proceedings may be admitted as evidence by a Court Martial, in cases not capital, or extending to the dismission of an officer, provided that the circumstances are such, that oral testimony cannot be obtained. But as Courts of Inquiry may be perverted to dishonorable purposes, and may be considered as engines of destruction to military merit, in the hands of weak and envious commandants, they are hereby prohibited, unless directed by the President of the United States, or demanded by the accused.

Art. 93. The Judge Advocate, or recorder, shall administer to the members the following oath:

"You shall well and truly examine and inquire, according to your evidence, into the matter now before you, without partiality, favor, affection, prejudice, or hope of reward. So help you God."

After which the President shall administer to the Judge Advocate, or recorder, the following oath:

"You, A B, do swear, that you will, according to your best abilities, accurately and impartially record the proceedings of the Court, and the evidence to be given in the case in hearing. So help you God."

The witnesses shall take the same oath as witnesses sworn before a Court Martial.

ART. 94. When any Commissioned officer shall die or be killed in the service of the United States, the Major of the regiment or the officer doing the Major's duty in his absence, or in any post or garrison, the second officer in command, or the Assistant Military Agent, shall immediately secure all his effects or equipage, then in camp or quarters, and shall make an inventory thereof, and forthwith transmit the same to the office of the Department of War, to the end, that his executors or administrators may receive the same.

ART. 95. When any non-commissioned officer or soldier shall die or be killed in the service of the United States, the then Commissioned officer of the troop or company, shall, in the presence of two other Commissioned officers, take an account of what effects he died possessed of, above his arms and accoutrements, and transmit the same to the office of the Department of War; which said effects are to be accounted for, and paid to the representatives of such deceased non-commissioned officer or soldier. And in case any of the officers, so authorized to take care of the effects of deceased officers and soldiers, should, before they have accounted to their representatives for the same, have occasion to leave the regiment or post, by preferment, or otherwise, they shall, before they be permitted to quit the same, deposite in the hands of the Commanding officer, or of the Assistant Military Agent, all the effects of such deceased non-commissioned officers and soldiers, in order that the same may be secured for, and paid to their respective representatives.

ART. 96. All officers, conducters, gunners, mattrosses,

drivers, or other persons whatsoever, receiving pay or hire in the service of the artillery or corps of engineers of the United States, shall be governed by the aforesaid Rules and Articles, and shall be subject to be tried by Courts Martial, in like manner with the officers and soldiers of the other troops in the service of the United States.

Art. 97. The officers and soldiers of any troops, whether militia or others, being mustered and in pay of the United States, shall, at all times and in all places, when joined or acting in conjunction with the regular forces of the United States, be governed by these Rules and Articles of War, and shall be subject to be tried by Courts Martial, in like manner with the officers and soldiers in the regular forces; save only that such Courts Martial shall be composed entirely of militia officers.

Art. 98. All officers serving by commission from the authority of any particular State, shall, on all detachments, Courts Martial, or other duty wherein they may be employed in conjunction with the regular forces of the United States, take rank next after all officers of the like grade in said regular forces, notwithstanding the commissions of such militia or State officers may be elder than the commissions of the officers of the regular forces of the United States.

Art. 99. All crimes not capital, and all disorders and neglects which officers and soldiers may be guilty of, to the prejudice of good order and military discipline, though not mentioned in the foregoing Articles of War, are to be taken cognizance of by a General or Regimental Court Martial, according to the nature and degree of the offence, and be punished at their discretion.

Art. 100. The President of the United States shall have power to prescribe the uniform of the Army.

Art. 101. The foregoing Articles are to be read and published once in every six months, to every garrison, regiment, troop, or company, mustered or to be mustered in the service of the United States, and are to be duly observed and obeyed by all officers and soldiers who are, or shall be, in said service.

Sec. 2. *And be it further enacted,* That in time of war, all persons not citizens of or owing allegiance to the United States of America, who shall be found lurking as spies, in or about the fortifications or encampments of the Armies of the United States, or any of them, shall suffer death, according to the law and usage of nations, by sentence of a General Court Martial.

Sec. 3. *And be it further enacted,* That the Rules and Regulations by which the Armies of the United States have her tofore been governed, and the resolves of Congress thereunto annexed, and respecting the same, shall henceforth be void and of no effect, except so far as may relate to any transactions under them, prior to the promulgation of this act, at the several posts and garrisons respectively, occupied by any part of the Army of the United States.

Approved, April 10, 1806.

EXTRACTS FROM ACTS OF CONGRESS HAVING REFERENCE TO THE ARTICLES OF WAR.

1. If any non-commissioned officer, musician, or private, shall desert the service of the United States, he shall, in addition to the penalties mentioned in the Rules and Articles of War, be liable to serve for and during such a period as shall, with the time he may have served previous to his desertion, amount to the full term of his enlistment; and such soldier shall and may be tried by a Court Martial and punished, although the term of his enlistment may have elapsed previous to his being apprehended or tried.—*Act 16th March*, 1802, *Sec.* 18.

2. No officer or soldier in the Army of the United States shall be subject to the punishment of death for desertion in time of peace.—*Act 29th May*, 1830.

3. So much of the "Act for establishing Rules and Articles for the government of the Armies of the United States," as authorizes the infliction of corporeal punishment by stripes or lashes, shall be, and the same is hereby, repealed.—*Act 16th May*, 1812, *Sec.* 7.

4. The seventh section of the act entitled "An act making further provision for the Army of the United States," passed on the sixteenth of May, one thousand eight hundred and twelve, shall be, and the same is hereby, repealed, so far as it applies to any enlisted soldier who shall be convicted by a General Court Martial of the crime of desertion. — *Act 2d March*, 1833, *Sec.* 7.

5. Whenever a general officer commanding an Army, or a Colonel commanding a separate department, shall be the accuser or prosecutor of any officer in the Army of the United States, under his command, the General Court Martial for the trial of such officer shall be appointed by the President of the United States.—*Act 29th May*, 1830, *Sec.* 1.

6. The proceedings and sentence of the said Court shall be sent directly to the Secretary of War, to be by him laid before the President, for his confirmation or approval, or orders in the case.—*Act 29th May*, 1830, *Sec.* 2.

7. So much of the sixty-fifth article of the first section of "An act for establishing Rules and Articles for the government of the Armies of the United States," passed on the tenth of April, eighteen hundred and six, as is repugnant hereto, shall be, and the same is hereby, repealed.—*Act 29th May*, 1830, *Sec.* 3.

8. Whenever a General Court Martial shall be ordered, the President of the United States may appoint some fit person to act as Judge Advocate, and in cases where the President shall not have made such appointment, the Brigadier-General or the President of the Court may make the same.—*Act 16th March*, 1802, *Sec.* 21.

INDEX.

A.

ARTICLES OF WAR.

B.

C.

ARTICLES OF WAR.

D.

ARTICLES OF WAR.

E.

ARTICLES OF WAR.

F.

APPENDIX.

ARTICLES OF WAR.

G.

ARTICLES OF WAR.

H.

ARTICLES OF WAR.

I.

ARTICLES OF WAR.

L.

ARTICLES OF WAR.

M.

ARTICLES OF WAR.

P.

ARTICLES OF WAR.

Q.

ARTICLES OF WAR.

R.

ARTICLES OF WAR.

S.

ARTICLES OF WAR.

T.

ARTICLES OF WAR.

THE END.